Open for Debate

Censorship

Open for Debate

Censorship

Ted Gottfried

BACON ACADEMY LMC

Marshall Cavendish
Benchmark
New York

For my son Dan, without whose computer wizardry this book would be in Limbo. I am grateful to personnel of the New York Central Research Library, the Mid-Manhattan Library, and the Queensboro Public Library for aid in gathering material for this book. Also, gratitude and much love to my wife, Harriet Gottfried, who—as always—read and critiqued this book. Her help was invaluable, but any shortcomings in the work are mine alone.

With special thanks to Stephanie Elizondo Griest of the Youth Free Expression Network, for her expert review of this manuscript.

Marshall Cavendish Benchmark
99 White Plains Road
Tarrytown, NY 10591
www.marshallcavendish.us

All Internet sites were available and accurate when sent to press.

Library of Congress Cataloging-in-Publication Data
Gottfried, Ted.
Censorship / by Ted Gottfried.—1st ed.
p. cm.—(Open for debate)
Includes bibliographical references and index.
ISBN 0-7614-1883-0
1. Censorship—United States—Popular works. I. Title. II. Series.
KF4775.Z9G68 2005
363.31'0973—dc22
2004021818

Photo research by Linda Sykes Picture Research, Inc., Hilton Head, SC

Cover: Royalty-free/Corbis

Royalty-Free/Corbis: 1, 2, 5, 6, 11, 116; Viviane Moos/Corbis: 16; Bettmann/Corbis: 32; Corbis: 35; Robert Galbraith/Reuters/Corbis: 40; The Kobal Collection: 54; Joe Skipper/Reuters/Corbis: 68; Pierre Ducharme/Reuters/Corbis: 86; Austrian Archives/Corbis: 91; Reuters/Corbis: 93; Reuters/Corbis: 96; Back Bay Books/ Little, Brown and Company, Time Warner Book Group: 103; Mark Peterson/Corbis: 108.

Printed in China
135642

Contents

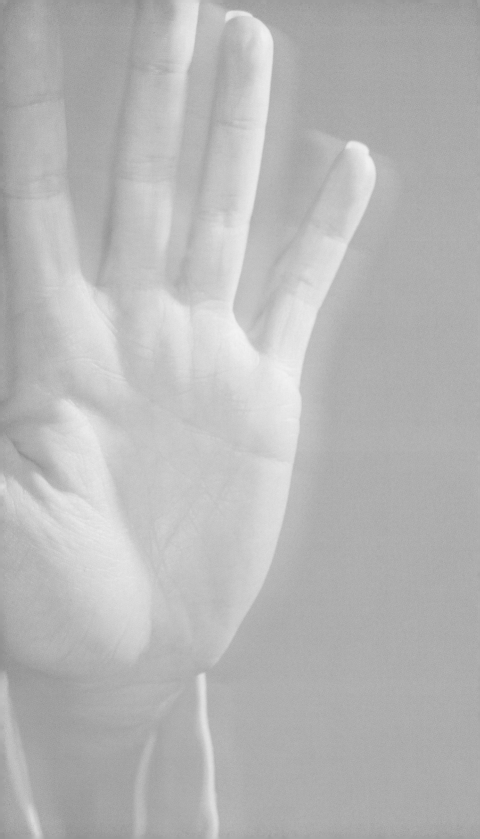

Foreword

Opinions on what constitutes censorship vary widely.
When a publisher decides not to publish a book for reasons
of morality, politics, or pressure from outside sources, some
would consider that censorship. However, the publisher is
investing money to produce the work, and anticipates a return on that investment. Doesn't that give the publisher the
right to decide what will, or will not, be produced?

When an editor says the author must make changes
because his or her view of the material differs from the
writer's, some call that censorship. It's the editor's job to
shape the material for publication, but where does shaping
the author's work end and changing it begin?

The bookseller has a limited amount of space to display his wares. The bookstore is in business to sell books.
When the store's racks display what may be trendy rather
than what may be controversial or literary, some people
consider that censorship.

Librarians have a limited budget to buy books. Circulation—how many books patrons take out—may be one of
the factors that determines the amount of money provided
to a library. When popular novels appear on library shelves

and serious nonfiction is in scarce supply, some call that censorship.

Should books be removed from school libraries because they contain language that some find objectionable? What if they include words that insult people on the basis of race, religion, ethnic background, or sexual preference? Who should decide? Teachers? Parents? The school board? The students?

How about freedom of speech? Does it include the right to verbally insult ethnic or racial groups? What if it leads to violence? Do schools and colleges have the right to institute speech codes to limit hate speech? Should they be able to enforce dress codes which forbid t-shirts with protest messages? Is symbolic speech—the right to burn a flag or the right to burn a cross—covered by free speech rights?

Among the media that might be censored are books, magazines, and newspapers. And what of modern technology? Should V-chips be used to block adult programs on television, or offensive Web sites on the Internet? Who determines what is offensive? Minors are barred from some movies because of portrayals of sex and violence deemed inappropriate by rating boards composed of people they don't know. Is that appropriate protection of children and young adults?

Most people believe that censorship is—at least in certain situations at certain times—a legitimate function of government. For example, most agree that sensitive material must be withheld from the public because of the need for national security. But where do legitimate security concerns leave off and politics or cover-ups begin? How much time should elapse before "TOP SECRET" documents are declassified? Should the papers of past presidents be released to the public? Are the secret tribunals and the secret testimony of the war on terrorism justified, or are they a violation of the free speech provisions of the Constitution? Official censorship sometimes conflicts with constitutional rights. Which should prevail?

These are some of the questions discussed in this book. There are many legitimate opinions. Whatever your view of censorship—whether you think it is always a bad thing, or believe it is necessary at times for a variety of reasons—this work will provide you with insights into other points of view.

Restricting the Internet

A fourteen-year-old boy sits down at a computer terminal in the young adult section of the children's room of a Midwestern public library. He surfs the Internet, finds what he wants, and moves slowly from picture to picture. He is too engrossed in what he is seeing to notice the seven-year-old who has wandered away from his mother and is staring at the screen from behind him.

The mother comes over to see what her child is gaping at. She sees a series of images of two naked adolescents having sex. She pulls her small child away and indignantly reports the pictures on the computer screen to the librarian. She demands that the librarian do something about it.

Exactly what will be done may depend on the individual librarian, or on the local community board which determines library policy. The board, or the librarian who is responsible to the board, may follow the position taken by the American Library Association (ALA). According to the

THE DEBATE CONTINUES OVER WHETHER SCHOOL AND PUBLIC LIBRARIANS SHOULD CENSOR WHAT MINORS ARE ABLE TO VIEW ON THEIR INTERNET SCREENS.

ALA, "parents and only parents have the right and responsibility to restrict their own children's access—and only their own children's access—to library resources, including the Internet." The ALA states that "publicly supported libraries are governmental institutions subject to the First Amendment, which forbids them from restricting information based on viewpoint or content discrimination." However, individual librarians and boards are free to disagree, and to limit access to objectionable material on library computers. Public schools are also free to limit or not limit computer use in keeping with local school board decisions.

The Communications Decency Act

The battle over how to deal with computer-accessed pornography began in earnest in the early 1990s when Enough Is Enough, an organization of anti-obscenity activists headed by Donna Rice Hughes, compiled a collection of objectionable material available on the Internet. The collection, known as The Blue Book, included descriptions of obscene matter and pornographic pictures. On June 5, 1995, The Blue Book was brought to the Democratic senator from Nebraska, James Exon. He circulated it among other senators.

This resulted in the Communications Decency Act (CDA), passed by a 91-to-5 vote of the Senate in 1995. CDA made it a crime to present indecent material on the Internet where children might see it. (Definitions of obscenity, pornography, and indecency differ widely, so the act defines indecency as any material that violates "community standards of morality and decency.") Despite the large majority, some legislators had their doubts. Congressman Newt Gingrich, at that time Speaker of the U.S. House of Representatives, said the act was "clearly a violation of free speech and it is a violation of the rights of adults to communicate with each other."

When the American Civil Liberties Union (ACLU), which traditionally opposes any restrictions on free speech, sued to challenge CDA, a 1997 decision by the United States Supreme Court found the law unconstitutional. The Court said it restricted speech on the Internet that was protected by the First Amendment. Writing for the Court, Justice John Paul Stevens called the wide prohibitions of the law "wholly unprecedented." He added that they were a "blanket restriction on speech."

Defining Objectable Material

Donna Rice Hughes, president of the anti-smut organization Enough Is Enough, presents the following shorthand explanations of the legal definitions used in judging objectionable books, photographs, movies, and other products made available by the pornography industry.

OBSCENITY
"Hard-core" graphic material that is obsessed with sex and/or sexual violence, obviously offensive, and lacking in serious value.

CHILD PORNOGRAPHY
Material picturing children under eighteen engaging in sexual activity: primarily an underground cottage industry. It is a crime scene record of a child's sexual abuse.

HARMFUL TO MINORS
Materials sold or displayed to children under eighteen that is unhealthy or unwholesome, obviously not suitable, and lacking in serious value for children.

BROADCAST INDECENCY
Includes messages or pictures on telephone, radio, or broadcast television that are offensive; descriptions or depictions of graphic sexual conduct.

EROTIC & SEMI-NUDE
"Soft-core" widely and readily available commercially.

The Child Pornography Prevention Act

Between the time that Congress passed the CDA and the Supreme Court struck it down, the 1996 Child Pornography Prevention Act (CPPA) had also become law. It was designed to update several previous laws passed by Congress that dealt with child pornography, but not specifically with the Internet. It not only banned from the Internet portrayals of sex involving real-life children under age eighteen, it also banned computer-generated images of children. Sponsors of the act had argued that children viewing these images would think they were real children and might mimic them.

CPPA had zeroed in on the technological advances in computer science. Using a computer technique known as *morphing*, moviemakers could create and alter images of adults having sex so that they looked like children. Under this law, those who did so could be sentenced to up to fifteen years in prison.

The Free Speech Coalition, a California trade association for the adult entertainment industry, challenged CPPA in federal court. Following verdicts in lower courts, the U.S. Supreme Court struck down the law on April 16, 2002. The Court found that the law "prohibits speech that records no crime and no victims by its production" even though it might be offensive. The justices found that the way the law was worded could make even adult actors portraying children in *Romeo and Juliet* guilty of breaking it. In a dissenting opinion, Chief Justice William Rehnquist insisted that CPPA was only "extending the definition of child pornography to reach computer-generated images that are virtually indistinguishable from real children engaged in sexually explicit conduct."

Values in Conflict

Though the CDA and CPPA were initially rejected by the Supreme Court, the CPPA was amended in 2003 so that it could be enforced if real children were involved. Advocates of Internet obscenity laws still press their case hard. Donna Rice Hughes points out that "there are laws to protect minors from indecency in the real world, but we don't have any such laws online. What we want is to put a virtual cellophane wrapper on the Internet." Such action would, of course, affect computer use in schools and libraries, as well as on home personal computers.

Opponents of such legislation are equally determined. ACLU attorney Ann Beeson believes that when it comes to passing laws to limit pornography on the Internet, "there is no way to do it right. The First Amendment limits have been set and the Supreme Court will enforce {those limits} every time."

Her point may well have revealed the heart of the matter. Which is the greater risk: exposing children to pornography or limiting the First Amendment rights of adult Internet users?

Cyberspace Predators

For concerned parents, it's no contest. Their greatest fear is that lack of control over Internet content may expose their children to pedophiles—adults who sexually exploit children. A two-month investigation by the *Maine Sunday Telegram* in 1998 uncovered an organization of pedophiles who "have joined together to build massive support networks online that encourage adult-child sex." In Keene, New Hampshire, police investigation of the Internet resulted in the arrests of fifteen men. They had come to

ADULTS MASQUERADING AS TEENAGERS HAVE PERSUADED UNDERAGE GIRLS AND BOYS TO MEET THEM FOR SEX. THIS INTERNET THREAT HAS LED SOME PARENTS TO CALL FOR AN INCREASE IN VIGILANCE OF ONLINE SITES FREQUENTED BY TEENS.

Keene to have sex with children ensnared on the Internet. They had traveled there from such far-off places as Norway, Holland, Canada, Georgia, Pennsylvania, New York, and other states.

Starting in 2002, FBI agents have been posing as teenage girls to snare pedophiles on the Internet. By 2003, this led to the conviction of 2,200 people across the United States for swapping child pornography or arranging to meet minors, according to a *Washington Post* report.

Many Internet pedophiles travel long distances for their prey, and many are repeat sex crime offenders. Ian Waddup, a British child molester, had three convictions for sex offenses against children under thirteen years of age. He was arrested in Cincinnati, Ohio, while taking a fifteen-year-old girl he had met over the Internet to a hotel room. Judge Sylvia Hendon told Waddup that "what you've done is found the most insidious way to creep into people's homes."

"I can go online as a fourteen-year-old, and can get a sexual solicitation in less than a minute," says police investigator Sgt. Andy Russell. "There's a motivated offender community out there that uses online technology to find kids for sex," adds Justice Department official Mike Medaris. "That we do know because we've locked up a lot of them." Some Internet chat rooms are named so that it's clear they are "are hangouts for men seeking sex with young girls." Predators are "master seducers," says Reuben Rodriguez, director of the exploited children's unit at the National Center for Missing and Exploited Children. "They manipulate children very, very easily."

Nevertheless, David Finkelhor, director of the Crimes Against Children Research Center, has concluded that the Internet threat "seems to be exaggerated in the media. Compared with other ways that young people are sexually victimized," Internet-related sex crimes against minors

17

National Research Council Findings

In 1998, the Protection of Children from Sexual Predators Act became federal law. One of its provisions directed the National Research Council to conduct a study of Internet pornography "in order to develop possible amendments to federal criminal law and other law enforcement techniques to respond to the problem." The investigation was headed by U.S. Attorney General Richard Thornburgh. The NRC report was released on May 2, 2002.

A preface to the findings by Thornburgh predicted that it would "disappoint those who expect a technological 'quick fix' to the challenge of pornography on the Internet." The study concluded that "no single approach—technical, legal, economic, or educational—will be sufficient. Rather, an effective framework for protecting our children from inappropriate materials and experiences on the Internet will require a balanced composite of all these elements." The report stressed the importance of the role of parenting and education "to reduce the number of children who are strongly motivated to obtain inappropriate sexually explicit materials."

Anti-filter proponent Judith Krug of the American Library Association interpreted the report as confirming that "filters are not going to be the solution." Internet anti-porn advocates, while not happy with the report, pointed out that it did not rule out the use of filters. Both sides were left with their points of view and few hard facts when committee members could not agree on just what impact sexually explicit material has on minors.

"appear to be uncommon." But even one crime is too many for those whose children are affected. For example, a thirteen-year-old Colorado girl was picked up in front of her school and sexually assaulted by a man she had met online.

The Child Online Protection Act

Reacting to incidents such as the assault on the Colorado girl, Internet censorship advocates persuaded Congress to pass the 1998 Child Online Protection Act (COPA). This new law was more narrowly focused than the two that preceded it.

Targeting Internet sites dealing with so-called objectionable adult material, COPA required the sites to obtain a credit card number or other proof of age before allowing users to look at material believed harmful to minors. The law called for criminal penalties and fines of as much as $50,000 a day.

COPA was challenged by a coalition including the ACLU; the Electronic Privacy Information Center, a public interest research center in Washington, D.C., focused on protecting First Amendment rights; and the Center for Democracy and Technology, an advocacy group that seeks to protect free speech on the Internet. The coalition suit charged that COPA violated the First and Fifth amendments to the Constitution. It claimed that "COPA places unconstitutional burdens on a wide category of protected speech while failing to achieve its goal of protecting children." The coalition pointed out that movies and television shows on the Internet risked restriction. It concluded that COPA "will not effectively prevent children from seeing inappropriate material originating from outside the U.S.," or receiving it through chat rooms or e-mail.

Some who favored Internet censorship were also not

happy with COPA. Bruce Taylor, a former federal prosecutor and anti-obscenity activist with the National Law Center for Children, said that COPA was "so weak that what it actually does is effectively legalize child computer porn" because the regulations are unenforceable.

Hearings in two federal courts resulted in an injunction barring enforcement of COPA. They said that by relying on "community standards" the law set too broad a condition for identifying harmful material. The Supreme Court reversed this decision, but ordered the lower court to reconsider other aspects of COPA's constitutionality. "Community standards" had been a legal basis for judging obscenity since 1973. Although COPA is still in effect, many prosecutors are reluctant to try Internet pornography cases because the law's provisions are so vague.

No Blocks, No Bucks!

Two years after COPA was passed, Congress enacted the 2000 Children's Internet Protection Act (CIPA) requiring public libraries and schools with Internet access to filter content harmful to minors, such as pornography and Web sites in which children are displayed in a sexual manner. The penalty for not filtering was a loss of federal funding. This federal money is administered under the Schools and Libraries Universal Service Fund, popularly known as the E-Rate. The E-Rate was created as part of the Telecommunications Act of 1996 to enable schools and libraries to afford access to modern telecommunications services such as the Internet. The E-Rate may dispense as much as $2.25 billion annually. Much of the money is given as discounts to libraries for the costs of telecommunications services. Without it, many libraries and schools in inner city and poor rural areas would not be able to offer Internet services.

Passage of CIPA brought to a head the ongoing conflict over the use of filters to block Internet pornography on computers available to the public. Judith F. Krug, director of the American Library Association's Office for Intellectual Freedom, spelled out the ALA's position in no uncertain terms. "Blocking material leads to censorship," she asserted. "That goes for pornography . . . too. If you don't like it, don't look at it." She told members of Enough is Enough that "if you don't want your children to access that information, you had better be with your children when they use a computer."

ALA's position was characterized by Internet censorship advocate Scott Weinberg as an "extremist attitude putting power and profits ahead of the special needs of children." Others agreed. Tanya L. Green, a lawyer associated with Concerned Women for America, wrote that ALA opposition to Internet filtering might result in "your neighborhood library becoming a breeding ground for sexual predators." She added that "for the sake of 'intellectual freedom,' the association is willing to put patrons, including children, in harm's way."

In a 2000 report written for the Family Research Council, a Judeo-Christian religious organization that promotes family values, former librarian David Burt wrote that while 74 percent of public libraries provide Internet access, only 15 percent of these use porn-blocking filters. His investigation also came up with "472 incidents of children accessing pornography, 106 incidents of adults exposing children to pornography, 5 incidents of attempted molestation, 41 incidents of the access of child pornography {and} 23 incidents of pornography being left for children."

The ALA's Judith Krug was not impressed. "Their number is so small that it is almost laughable," she responded. She added that "only one child out of a trillion billion" might access porn via a library computer.

The American Library Association Position

The Freedom to Read Statement released jointly by the American Library Association (ALA) and the Association of American Publishers argues that preparing young people "to meet the diversity of experiences in life to which they will be exposed" is not accomplished by keeping them from "works for which they are not prepared. In these matters, taste differs, and taste cannot be legislated; nor can machinery be devised which will suit the demands of one group without limiting the freedom of others." The statement grants "that ideas can be dangerous; but that the suppression of ideas is fatal to a democratic society." It concludes that "freedom itself is a dangerous way of life, but it is ours."

In opposing librarian oversight of the Internet—including filters designed to block out objectionable material—the ALA cites Amendment I of the Bill of Rights, more familiarly known as the First Amendment to the United States Constitution, and Amendment IX, which they believe supports their view of Amendment I. The relevant portion of Amendment I says that "Congress shall make no law . . . abridging the freedom of speech, or of the press . . ." Amendment IX, in its entirety, reads as follows: "The enumeration in the Constitution, of certain rights, shall not be construed to deny or disparage others retained by the people."

Those who disagree with the ALA believe that the framers of the Constitution could never have anticipated a worldwide Internet, and never meant this to apply to the dissemination of pornography on it.

Filters and Fallout

Filter advocates were worried that children using search engines might accidentally be connected to pornography sites. They cited examples in which putting such words as cat, rooster, or tool into search engines had objectionable results. Anti-filter forces, on the other hand, pointed out that by screening out obscene language and other words associated with pornography, filters would also block useful material. The word "mating," for instance, might block out sites dealing with biology as well as graphic portrayals of sex.

Ultimately, such questions came down to the effectiveness of filters. Krug says flatly that "filters don't work." Supporters of CIPA concede that filters can't stop 100 percent of undesirable content, but claim such a standard is unrealistic. They note that the Food and Drug Administration would never be able to approve any product if it had to be 100 percent satisfactory.

This argument would turn out to be the deciding factor in the case brought by the ALA and the ACLU challenging CIPA. In May 2002, a three-judge federal district court in Philadelphia decided unanimously that CIPA was unconstitutional because filters don't work. Applauding the decision, an editorial in the *San Jose Mercury News* said the court had concluded "they don't work because they allow some porn sites to go unfiltered. But more important, they don't work because they block thousands of sites that contain no sexually explicit material, such as a site for a Buddhist nun and one belonging to the Knights of Columbus. As such, a federal requirement to impose filters in libraries violates First Amendment protections."

As a result of the district court's decision, the government was forbidden to withhold funds from libraries that did not install filters. The decision was appealed to the Supreme Court by the Justice Department. On November 12, 2002, the Court agreed to consider the case. On June 23, 2003, the Supreme Court in *ALA* v. *U.S.* reversed the district court. In a 6-to-3 decision, the Court held that public libraries must purchase filtering software and comply with all parts of the CIPA.

Hate Blockers

Attempts to use filters on the Internet have not been limited to anti-pornography campaigns. In 1998, Cyber Patrol, a division of the Learning Company in Cambridge, Massachusetts, developed a so-called hate filter for installation on the Internet by the Anti-Defamation League (ADL). According to ADL spokesman Howard Berkowitz's testimony before the U.S. Senate Committee on the judiciary, there are "hundreds of bigotry-laden sites on the Web" which "target the young [and are] aimed at influencing both attitudes and behavior." (The Simon Wiesenthal Center, an international Jewish human rights center, puts the number at more than 1,500.) Some hate-mongering organizations, Berkowitz testified, "such as the World Church of the Creator, have posted Web sites filled with simple propaganda devoted specifically to wooing children."

Denying the Holocaust in which six million Jews were slaughtered by the Nazis is frequently a starting point for Internet hate sites. From there, a web of links may lead the young viewer to visual stereotypes of Jews, blacks, gays, Asians, Muslims, and other minorities. Other links include computer games in which the purpose is to shoot, kill, or maim caricatured stereotypes. Accompanying language dehumanizes the targets. Propaganda verging on campaigns for genocide prevails throughout these links.

A Ku Klux Klan Web site denies the Holocaust in order to attract young people to their cause of re-imposing segregation on African Americans, as well as urging persecution of Jews, Catholics, and others. The purpose of Holocaust denial, according to an e-mail message sent out to the mailing list of the National Socialist White People's Party, is "to make National Socialism an acceptable political alternative again." National Socialism is another name for Nazism.

When the ADL filter is installed, the user accessing such sites will see a "Hate Zone. Access Restricted" message on the screen. The viewer is then directed to an ADL "Stop Hate" site. Here, he or she will be offered information about various forms of bigotry.

The ACLU opposes such filters on principle, pointing out that "to justify suppression of speech, the speech must be intended to produce imminent lawless action and must be likely to produce such action." It is difficult to prove that hate sites spark such action. Librarian-author Karen G. Schneider believes the ADL filters are counter-productive— like forbidden fruit. "There's nothing to make a bad idea look silly," she points out, "like putting it out in the cold, hard light of day."

Blocking hate sites and filtering out pornography sites bring up different kinds of questions. However, the one issue raised in both cases is to what degree a limit on Internet content clashes with the First Amendment right of free speech. Is such a limitation ever justified? Should the hate-mongers and the pornography purveyors be granted absolute liberty to spread their material? This is the issue that will be continue to be debated as we navigate the boundaries of the Internet.

2

Morality or Prudery?

The satirical play *Lysistrata* was written by Aristophanes in 411 BCE. Its theme concerns the ending of the Peloponnesian War by Athenian women who deny their husbands sexual relations until the fighting stops. Lysistrata, the organizer of the protest, has a naked woman display herself to the two armies in order to hasten the war's end. The frustrated Athenians and Spartans then quickly make peace and return to their wives. *Lysistrata* is a classic.

In 1954, the United States Post Office seized a rare illustrated edition of *Lysistrata* en route from England to a Los Angeles bookseller. The seizure of the book was in keeping with a law banning pornographic material from the U.S. mails. The law, known as the Comstock Act, had been passed in 1873. While most provisions of the act dealing with birth control and abortion have been repealed, the Comstock Act is still part of federal law.

Sanitizing the Bible

Censorship of so-called pornographic material pre-dates the writing of *Lysistrata*. One of the crimes for which the Greek philosopher Socrates was put to death circa 339 BCE was "corrupting the morals of the young" in his lectures. In 213 BCE, illustrated, hand-written pornographic scrolls were ruled taboo by the Emperor Shih Huang-ti of China. The punishment for possessing them was branding by hot irons followed by a sentence of hard labor.

Later, following the invention of the printing press in the fifteenth century, both the Bible and the works of Shakespeare were censored to remove offensive language. In 1818, in England, Thomas Bowdler of the Society for the Suppression of Vice, issued *The Family Shakespeare,* a version of the plays from which much of the bawdy language and references to immoral behavior had been removed. Actually, Bowdler admired Shakespeare tremendously. He believed that by censoring the plays he was making them more accessible to those who otherwise might have been offended by them. Today, these bowdlerized versions of Shakespeare's works are the plays that are almost always published or performed.

In 1833, dictionary-maker Noah Webster decided that the Bible contained "many words and phrases . . . so offensive, especially to females, as to create a reluctance in young persons to attend Bible classes and schools in which they are required to read passages which cannot be repeated without a blush." He removed entire sections because they were "beyond the reach of effective bowdlerization." He also changed words he thought might give rise to impure thoughts.

Ancient Erotica

Both Bowdler and Webster believed they were acting from the best of motives. It was a time when impure thoughts were believed to threaten a person's immortal soul. Pornography was believed to be the writings of Satan. But what is pornography?

It seems to have existed since the dawn of time. Among the earliest drawings on the walls of caves were depictions of bodily functions and erotic activities that even by today's standards might be termed pornographic. Stick figures of Stone Age men and women having sex have been found on cave walls in France. They date back approximately 40,000 years. Excavations in Mesopotamia dating back to 3000 BCE revealed representations of lovemaking. "Spring coins" from the Chinese Han Dynasty (206 BCE–220 BCE) portrayed people making love. These were given to children "as a form of protection against supernatural forces."

Ancient Hindu temples of India were adorned with sexually graphic ivory carvings. Classic Greek sculptures, coins, pottery and tapestries reveal that "sex was worshiped as sacred in the Mediterranean regions." Primitive Mayan vases discovered in Peru were shaped like men's sex organs. In ancient Japan sexual art exaggerated both size and activity.

Many of these artifacts are regarded today as primitive art. Where art leaves off and pornography begins has always been a subject of controversy for censors and those who protest censorship. Always, at the heart of the dispute, is the same question: what is pornography?

The Price of Pornography

The *Encyclopaedia Britannica* defines pornography as "the representation of erotic behavior . . . intended to cause sexual excitement." It goes on to explain that censorship of it is based "on at least one of the following assumptions":

(1) "pornography will tend to deprave or corrupt the morals of youth, or of adults and youth;

(2) "consumption of such matter is a cause of sexual crime."

Today's anti-pornography forces might add that pornography undermines family values and erodes the moral fiber of society.

They cite facts and figures to back up this claim, as follows:

- **The divorce rate in the United States is approximately 50 percent according to figures compiled in 2002 by the Census Bureau.**

- **The Centers for Disease Control (CDC) reported 857,475 abortions performed in 2000, the last year for which figures were compiled (but that was down from well over one million in 1996).**

- **The proportion of first babies conceived out of wedlock in the United States by young women in the 1990s has nearly tripled since the 1930s (again, that has gone down dramatically in the last few years).**

- **U.S. teens are more likely than adolescents in other industrialized countries to start having intercourse at fifteen years of age, and to have multiple sexual partners.**

- **Three million U.S. teens contract new cases of sexually transmitted diseases each year, a rate fifty to a hundred times higher than in other industrialized countries.**

• **Teen suicides have increased by 200 percent over the last forty years.**

• **In 2000, the U. S. Bureau of Justice reported that the nation's children were victims in 67 percent of sexual assaults including almost half of all rapes.**

• **The number of rapes in the United States is four times higher than in Germany, thirteen times higher than England, and twenty times higher than Japan (though, of course, their populations are very different).**

Although there is little or no evidence of a cause-and-effect relationship between pornography and divorce, teen sex, teen suicide, abortions, or rape, what these statistics add up to for anti-pornography advocates is a breakdown of the political and social morality of American society. Their concern is fueled by an increasingly erotic outpouring of material in magazines, on television, and in the movies. This fear, however, is not a new one. It was voiced over a hundred years ago by a man whose name would become synonymous with censorship.

"Comstockery"

The man was Anthony Comstock. In 1873, he became secretary of the newly formed New York Society for the Suppression of Vice. Over the next ten years the society would bring about 700 arrests, seize 27,856 pounds of allegedly

BACK IN THE 1890S, THE BOOKS OF BIRTH CONTROL ADVOCATE MARGARET SANGER WERE BANNED BECAUSE THEY WERE CONSIDERED LEWD. HERE, SHE HAS HER MOUTH COVERED IN PROTEST AT NOT BEING ALLOWED TO DISCUSS BIRTH CONTROL IN BOSTON.

lewd books, and destroy 64,836 "articles for immoral use," otherwise known as condoms. That same year, 1873, Comstock addressed Congress. "Tears flowed from his eyes" as he begged for "a law to stop the 'hydra-headed monster' of vice."

The Comstock Act passed. "What this bill did," as Congresswoman Patricia Schroeder a century later reminded the House of Representatives, was enable Comstock, acting alone, "to define what would be lewd, what would be filthy, or what would be things that should be banned. He was particularly upset about anything dealing with family planning and also any kind of abortion or contraceptive information." She recounted how the Congress "then commissioned him as a special agent of the Post Office and vested him with the powers of arrest and the privilege of free transportation so that he could go around and enforce this law unilaterally."

Comstock performed his duties as a special agent for the Post Office for forty-two years. Only his death in 1915 brought his crusade against pornography and other forms of vice to an end. During that time he succeeded in having Walt Whitman's classic book of poetry, *Leaves of Grass,* banned. The books of birth control advocate Margaret Sanger were also banned by Comstock, and he forced the closing of some of her clinics. He also led a successful campaign to halt performances of George Bernard Shaw's play about a prostitute, *Mrs. Warren's Profession.* The world-renowned Irish-British playwright called Comstock's anti-vice campaign a "joke," and coined the derogatory word "Comstockery" to describe outrageous censorship. Congresswoman Schroeder described how Comstock "went on to brag . . . that he had been responsible for enough criminal convictions of people to fill a sixty-one-coach passenger train."

Jailing the Jezebel

Victoria C. Woodhull was the first woman to run for president of the United States. She spent election eve of 1872 in a jail cell. Anthony Comstock put her there.

Long a leader in the struggle to obtain the right to vote for women, Woodhull was the candidate of the Equal Rights Party. Her political beliefs had their roots in her personal life. At the age of fourteen she married an abusive alcoholic. After getting a divorce, she became a vocal critic of the legal and religious principles that forced women to endure abusive marriages.

Because of Woodhull's lectures on what she called "social freedom," author Harriet Beecher Stowe, the renowned author of *Uncle Tom's Children*, spoofed her in one of her novels. "No woman that was not willing to be dragged through every kennel and slopped into every dirty pail of water like an old mop, would ever consent to run as a candidate," Stowe wrote. Stowe's brother, as it happened, was the Reverend Henry Ward Beecher.

On October 28, 1872, *Woodhull & Claflin's Weekly*, a journal partly owned and edited by Woodhull, ran an article detailing an adulterous affair between Reverend Beecher and Elizabeth Tilton, a member of his congregation. Theodore Tilton, her betrayed husband, admired Woodhull, and became her first biographer. The details of the affair appearing in the article so outraged Comstock that he demanded the New York City district attorney bring charges against Woodhull.

When the district attorney refused, Comstock, using an alias, wrote the publication requesting a copy of the article by mail. After he received it, he sent federal marshals to arrest Woodhull on a charge of sending obscene material through the postal service.

FEMINIST VICTORIA WOODHULL WAS JAILED IN 1872 FOR PUBLISHING THE DETAILS OF AN ADULTEROUS AFFAIR IN HER JOURNAL, *WOODHULL & CLAFLIN'S WEEKLY*.

Since sending obscene material through the mail is a national offense, he circumvented the local district attorney.

Woodhull spent weeks in various New York City jails, paid more than $600,000 in fines, and faced libel charges related to the Beecher scandal for nearly two weeks. In the end, she was found innocent of all charges.

The ordeal, however, had taken its toll. She fled to England, and the women's suffrage movement lost one of its most dedicated champions. It took almost forty more years for women to get the vote—in 1919. That was four years after the death of Comstock, who had opposed it to the very end.

September Morn

In 1878, Comstock encountered Madame Restell, a retired abortionist and sometime supplier of birth control items and literature. She was an old woman by the time she sold Comstock contraceptives and printed matter. Nevertheless, he had her arrested for dispensing articles used for "immoral" purposes. Fearing the publicity of a trial and the embarrassment it would cause her granddaughter, who had married into New York society, Madame Restell lowered herself into her bath and slit her throat with a carving knife. Her death received wide coverage in the newspapers, particularly after it was revealed that she had left an estate of over a million dollars—a tremendous amount of money for that time. The newspaper stories enhanced Comstock's reputation as a single-minded and serious anti-vice crusader.

Comstock's most famous case, a classic example of how aggressive censorship can backfire, involved a painting. The creation of French artist Paul Chabas, who titled his painting *Matinee de Septembre (September Morn)*, the work first appeared in the United States in the window of a Manhattan art gallery in May 1913. It depicted a side view of a naked young woman crouching in the waters of a cold lake. It was no more revealing than an advertisement one might find in the pages of a modern magazine. The shop in whose window it appeared was selling small reproductions of *September Morn* at ten cents apiece. They were not selling very well until publicist Harry Reichenbach was hired by the shop to promote sales.

Reichenbach called Comstock. He told the vice crusader that there was a lewd picture of a naked woman in a shop window. Adding that "little boys are gathering around there to look at her," Reichenbach gave him the address. When Comstick didn't respond, Reichenbach paid him a personal visit. He told Comstock that the picture was "undermining the morals of our city's youth!"

Finally, Comstock agreed to come to the shop. Reichenbach hired a group of young boys at fifty cents apiece to be there to greet him. When Comstock showed up, the boys began hooting and pointing at the picture and making lewd remarks. Comstock marched into the shop and ordered the owner to "Remove that picture!" The shopkeeper refused.

The New York Society for the Suppression of Vice brought charges against the shopkeeper for obscenity, but a court found him not guilty. The judge said the painting was innocent and no threat to the morality of youth. The publicity generated by the trial resulted in the sale of more than seven million copies of *September Morn*. Soon reproductions were appearing on calendars, postcards, candy boxes, bottle openers, and other objects. Eventually, *September Morn* was sold to the Metropolitan Museum of Art, where it still hangs. Following the resolution of the case, and for the rest of Comstock's life, he was the butt of jokes and comic songs heard on vaudeville stages throughout the United States and Great Britain.

Shifting Boundaries

Today, for the most part, Comstock's morality would be seen as extreme. At the time, however, most religious leaders and government officials applauded his war on vice. In the early twentieth century before the spread of Sigmund Freud's psychological theories on sexuality, before "girlie" magazines such as *Playboy* and *Hustler*, before mini-skirts and bikinis, before four-letter words could be heard on television, before nudity and sex scenes were common in movies and on cable television—before, in other words, the morality of the Victorian Era had eroded—Comstock was its living symbol.

He was backed by both state and federal laws. The full force of police agencies were at his command. Those whose writings, paintings, or speech Comstock found immoral faced jail. Those who sold works deemed lewd or lascivious faced not only prison but substantial fines. A generally agreed-upon morality was current throughout the land, and Comstock was its crusading knight in shining armor.

As the moral climate became less restrictive, however, the courts of the United States were forced to redefine what was permissible in literature, art, speech, and other areas. More permissive attitudes progressively changed the interpretation of the laws, and the new definitions liberalized behavior throughout the twentieth century. The debate on the effect of that liberalization continues.

3

See-Saw:
Smut and the Law

What can, and cannot, be censored often comes down to
the basic question of whether state and local laws or a national standard should prevail. Amendment X of the Bill
of Rights declares that "the powers not delegated to the
United States by the Constitution, nor prohibited by it to
the States, are reserved to the States respectively, or to the
people." Supreme Court justices who voted to uphold censorship decisions by lower courts often did so because they
were reluctant to challenge the rights of state courts in this
area. Those justices who opposed them believed state censorship was often in violation of the First Amendment.
Over the years, each of the fifty states has evolved its own
criteria for censorship.

Such criteria go back to before the American Revolution, when the states were British colonies. As early as
1712, the crown colony of Massachusetts declared it a
crime to publish any "filthy, obscene, or profane song,
pamphlet, libel or mock sermon." All of the states

CARMELLA DECESARE POSES AFTER BEING NAMED *PLAYBOY*'S PLAYMATE OF THE YEAR 2004. FEMINISTS HAVE LONG CONSIDERED "CHEESECAKE" AS PORNOGRAPHY THAT SHOULD BE BANNED, BUT CIVIL LIBERTARIANS SEE IT DIFFERENTLY.

presently have, or have had, obscenity laws. Between 1842 and 1956, twenty federal anti-pornography laws were passed by the U.S. Congress.

Inflaming the Reader

Most of these laws followed a principle laid down in the British Obscene Publications Act of 1857. This English statute, according to the *Encyclopaedia Britannica*, "was a precedent for U.S. anti-obscenity legislation." Among its first targets were translations of the novel *La Terre* (*The Soil*) by Emile Zola. Its English publisher, Henry Vizitelly, went to jail when it was determined that Zola's works had a "tendency" to "deprave and corrupt those whose minds are open to such immoral tendencies." What this established in American law was the principle that if one or two passages in a work aroused immoral tendencies in one or two people, the work could be banned as obscene. The work as a whole did not have to be pornographic, nor did the objectionable passages have to inspire such tendencies in all who read it. All it took was a couple of readers who were easily affected to prove the case for obscenity.

The great majority of these cases did not reach the Supreme Court. They were tried in state courts or in lower federal courts and guilty verdicts went unchallenged. In 1932, such a case was heard in federal court, and the result changed the criteria for determining obscenity. The case was *United States of America* v. *One Book Entitled Ulysses by James Joyce*.

Customs agents had seized a copy of *Ulysses* on the grounds that it was illegal to import obscene matter into the country. *Ulysses* had been published in 1922 in Paris, and its frankly erotic scenes had caused a sensation. The novel had been banned in many European cities and copies had been burned in James Joyce's native city of Dublin. In literary circles, however, it had been hailed as a masterpiece. Now, ten years later, Random House wanted to publish it in the United States. When the single copy was seized, Random House lawyers fought the obscenity charges brought by the customs department. The case was heard by federal Judge John M. Woolsey.

As in previous obscenity cases, Judge Woolsey applied the standard of a work tending "to stir the sex impulse, or to lead to impure and lustful thoughts." However, he imposed an additional, and very important, condition. He said that this reaction must apply to people "with average sex instincts," to "the man on the street." By this standard, he ruled, *Ulysses* was not pornographic. When the government appealed the decision and the U.S. Court of Appeals upheld Judge Woolsey's decision, it changed the criteria for future obscenity cases. Judge Augustus Hand, writing for the Appeals Court, established "that a publication of literary merit should not be judged obscene on the basis of particular passages taken out of context."

Roth v. United States

A further shift in the legal standards for determining pornography took place with the 1957 case of *Roth v. United States*. Samuel Roth was the publisher of *American Aphrodite*, a magazine devoted to erotica. Volume I, number 3, of the publication featured a sexually explicit excerpt from the banned book *Venus and Tannhauser*, by Aubrey Beardsley. The magazine was distributed through the mail, and Roth was charged with using the postal service to circulate obscene material.

When Roth was found guilty of distributing pornography, he appealed the case all the way up to the Supreme Court. Here his conviction was upheld by a vote of 6-to-3 and Roth—age sixty-two—was sentenced to prison for five years. The majority opinion, written by Justice William Brennan, spelled out the difference between sex and obscenity. "The portrayal of sex," he wrote, "is not itself sufficient reason to deny material the constitutional protection of freedom of speech and press." However, he added that the standard was "whether to the average person, applying contemporary standards, the dominant theme of the material taken as a whole applies to the prurient interest."

Lower federal courts, as well as state and local courts, looking to the Roth decision for guidance, were thrown into confusion. Some measured works according to their "dominant theme." Some read "contemporary standards" to mean local morality, which varied greatly from, say, New York City or Chicago, to rural Iowa or Maine. "Prurient interest" gave them the most trouble. Even among judges, what was prurient to one was merely distasteful, or even humorous, to another. Jury rooms rang with arguments between the offended and the permissive.

Packaging Cheesecake

Of the several attempts by the Supreme Court to deal with the confusion, the most generally accepted—if often misinterpreted—was the majority opinion written by Justice John M. Harlan in the 1962 case *Manual Enterprises v. Day*. Rewording the contemporary standards of the *Roth* decision, he defined "prurient interest" as works "so offensive on their face as to affront current community standards of decency." Harlan meant this to establish national standards, but it didn't correct the problem, and right up to the present, anti-pornography advocates insist that he meant local concepts of decency. Indeed, there have been many convictions based on this reading of "community standards."

Two years after *Manual Enterprises v. Day*, federal judge Potter Stewart (later to be appointed to the Supreme Court) heard the case against *The Lovers*, a French film being prosecuted as pornography. When Stewart decided against the ban, there was an outcry from those concerned with the relaxation of decency standards. Defending himself, Stewart confessed that while he was not pro-pornography, he could not really define it. Pressed, he added, "I know it when I see it." Those who favored liberalization of the laws regarding erotica often quoted this statement as an example of how pornography was a matter of taste, rather than morality.

That same year, Brennan wrote the majority Supreme Court opinion in *Jacobellis v. Ohio*. It came as a decided blow to Morality in Media and other groups trying to stem the flow of erotic material which had begun in the 1960s. Brennan wrote that for material to be judged obscene, or pornographic, it had to be "utterly without redeeming social importance."

The decision came just as *Playboy* was building to over a million circulation and spinning off countless imitators, such as *Gent* and *Bachelor* and *Escapade*. These so-called "skin magazines" leaped on the *Jacobellis* decision as providing them with a cover for their semi-nude displays. They began bracketing their cheesecake (as semi-nude pictures of women were called) with articles on current events and short fiction by well known authors.

One publisher, eager to avoid too-close scrutiny by the post office, came up with the idea of running the last names of serious writers on his magazine's cover in extra-large type with unrelated first names above in very small four-point type. Thus, the publication would have featured stories and articles by elmer MAILER, arnie KISSINGER, and hedy FRIEDAN. He was only dissuaded when the magazine's editor, backed up by the firm's lawyer, persuaded him that he could be sued for libel, or prosecuted for deliberately misleading advertising.

Issues of Race

During this period, while standards of pornography were being defined and redefined, the case of *Ginzburg v. United States* (1966) had been working its way through the lower courts to the Supreme Court. The accused was Ralph Ginzburg, a long-time distributor of erotic material who had been described as "a lewd and obnoxious man" with "an uncanny ability to go straight for the vulgar."

Testimony in his earlier trials, which would influence the higher court in his case, showed that he had sought mailing privileges for his magazine *Eros* from places whose names would provide titillating postmarks. One of the least suggestive of these was Intercourse, Pennsylvania.

Eros was packaged like an art book with a hard cover, glossy paper, and an oversized format with lots of white space to frame its elegant photographs and illustrations. Ginzburg called it "a magazine of sexual candor," and said that it had been made possible by "recent court decisions that have realistically interpreted America's obscenity laws." It had a readership of around 100,000.

The issue of *Eros* that resulted in the prosecution of Ginzburg contained a story by Guy de Maupassant (a renowned figure of French literature) illustrated by Edgar Degas, an article cautioning against lovemaking by people with weak hearts, photographs of male prostitutes soliciting in Bombay, reproductions of French postcards featuring topless models, an off-color essay by Mark Twain, some particularly suggestive selections from the Bible, and corny jokes like the one asking how porcupines make love (answer: carefully). All of this might have squeezed by the most recent Supreme Court standards, but the article that was focused on when government agents seized the magazine did not. It was an artistically stylized, but realistic

Going to the Movies

During the 1960s and 1970s, when cases involving the sexual content of movies came before the Supreme Court, time was set aside every week or two to view the films. The justices called this "movie day." Often the screenings were held in a basement storeroom of the Court building.

Burger did not attend these showings because he found the material offensive, though not necessarily illegal. Justices William O. Douglas and Hugo Black shunned them for a different reason. Black deplored the Court as a "Supreme Board of Censors," and expressed disapproval that men of an age when sexual prowess is in decline should render judgments about erotic subjects. "If I want to go to a film," Black said, "I should pay my money."

Justice Douglas refused to view obscenity or pornography in any form. He believed that the Court had erred in even considering obscenity or pornography an exception to the First Amendment. He agreed with Justice Thurgood Marshall, who had written that "if the First Amendment means anything, it means that a state has no business telling a man, sitting alone in his own house, what books he may read or what films he must watch."

Nevertheless, unlike Black and Douglas, Justice Marshall attended "movie day" and enjoyed it. Justice Harry Blackmun—stony-faced and disapproving—sat through such films as *I Am Curious Yellow* and *Sexual Freedom in Denmark*, featuring a variety of hard-core sex acts. Justices Marshall and Byron White and their clerks made quips about "redeeming social value" and "I know it when I see it" as they watched the films. The newest justice, Lewis Powell, simply sat and watched, his face expressionless. When the first showing he attended was over, he said he was shocked and disgusted. He had never seen such films and had no idea they were even made.

The different reactions by the justices during that period may have reflected disparities among public attitudes more than they realized. Tolerance of erotic material was growing with many people's disgust at its prevalence. Today, more than thirty years later, the twenty-first century still has not tipped the scales one way or the other. The clash between family values and the First Amendment right to view erotic material has yet to be resolved.

photographic essay showing a series of pictures of a naked black man and a naked white woman embracing.

They were not engaging in explicit sex, but to many people the photos seemed to confirm the myth of excessive male black sexuality embraced by racists. At this time the civil rights movement in America was in full swing. Entrenched bigots pointed to the photos to stir up fears of race-mixing. Some integrationists charged that the photographs were exploiting race as well as sex. The issue of just how obscene the pictures were—or weren't—was hopelessly blurred by issues of race. In 1966, the Supreme Court upheld the verdict finding Ginzberg guilty of distributing pornography and sentencing him to five years in prison, of which he only served eight months. The high court said that while *Eros* might not, of itself, be pornographic, it must be judged so "against a background of commercial exploitation of erotica solely for the sake of their prurient appeal." Justice Hugo Black dissented. In a minority opinion, Black wrote that Ginzburg had merely distributed "printed matter about sex which neither Ginzburg nor anyone else could possibly have known to be criminal."

The Triple Standard

The Ginzburg decision established that material about sex could be legally pornographic if advertised to attract the buyer's taste for lewdness. The following year, in *Redrup v. New York,* the Supreme Court said that convictions for obscenity were only valid if they were based on guarding juveniles or unwitting adults from salacious matter. These decisions, coming as close together as they did, brought protests from those on both sides of the censorship controversy.

In 1973, the Supreme Court tried to clarify matters in the case of *Miller v. California.* It listed three criteria for determining a work obscene and not protected by the First Amendment:

1) That the average person, applying contemporary community standards, would find that the work, taken as a whole, appeals to the prurient interest; and

2) That the work depicts or describes in a patently offensive way, as measured by contemporary community standards, sexual conduct specifically defined by the applicable law; and

3) That a reasonable person would find that the work, taken as a whole, lacks serious literary, artistic, political, and scientific value.

Those who wanted to outlaw pornography applauded the removal from these standards of the loophole which had said that to be pornographic, material had to be "utterly without redeeming social value." Also, Chief Justice Warren Burger assured them that community standards did not have to be national. A follow-up decision, *Paris Adult Theater I v. Slaton* (1973), relaxed the standards for declaring sexual material pornographic, saying that if it had an effect on family life or community welfare, that was reason enough for banning it.

Child Pornography

By the mid-1970s there had been what was labeled a sexual revolution in America. A more relaxed morality had

Women Against Pornography

In 1977, prominent feminist Robin Morgan wrote that "pornography is the theory, and rape is the practice." Two years later, Women Against Pornography was founded. It was the start of a major split in the women's movement, and the beginning of a campaign to pass laws outlawing pornography on the grounds that it incited men to commit sex crimes against women.

The leaders of the campaign were authors Andrea Dworkin and Catharine MacKinnon, who was also a law professor at the University of Michigan. MacKinnon had written that showing pornography to men was "like saying 'kill' to a trained guard dog." In 1983, the two women helped draft legislation for the city of Minneapolis, Minnesota, which labeled pornography "a practice of sex discrimination" and authorized lawsuits for damages against those who sold it, or coerced people into posing for it. The city council passed the legislation, but the mayor refused to sign it into law.

In 1984, a similar bill became law in Indianapolis, Indiana. It had the backing of such anti-feminist leaders as Phyllis Schlafly and other opponents of the women's rights movement. In opposition, the Feminist Anti-Censorship Taskforce and Feminists for Free Expression were organized. Leading feminists such as Betty Friedan and ACLU president Nadine Strossen also spoke out against this kind of anti-pornography legislation. Bitter conflict marked the "so-called sex wars within the feminist movement" that followed.

Eventually, the Indianapolis law was declared unconstitutional by a federal court. The Supreme Court upheld the decision. Dworkin brought a lawsuit against *Hustler* magazine in federal court, charging that pornography did not constitute free speech under the Constitution. She lost.

Meanwhile, Catharine MacKinnon had co-written a brief supporting anti-pornography legislation in Canada. It influenced the Canadian Supreme Court to declare pornography "degrading" and against the law. As an unintended result, two books authored by Andrea Dworkin were impounded by Canadian customs officials on charges of portraying "illegally eroticized pain and bondage."

The Pornography Victims Compensation Act, a MacKinnon-Dworkin inspired bill, became law in Illinois in 1993. Under its terms, rape victims and victims of other sexual assaults can sue producers or sellers of pornography on the grounds that it was a "substantial cause" of the crime. Similar legislation is being considered in Washington, Massachusetts, Wisconsin, California, and Suffolk County, New York, and a comparable bill was introduced in the U.S. Senate, but has not been passed.

taken hold. Once-banned language and acts of passion were now beginning to be heard and seen on movie screens, and even on television. The Supreme Court standards were being enforced less and less. One area, however, was already strictly taboo—child pornography. In 1982, the Supreme Court upheld a New York State law making its distribution a crime. In 1990, the Court ruled that a person who possessed or looked at child pornography in his or her own home could face prosecution. Not all the justices agreed. Justice Brennan pointed out that many works of art featured "models under eighteen years of age, and many acclaimed photographs and films have included nude or partially clad minors."

Concern with the victimizing of children used in the creation of child pornography, plus a mounting concern with the use of such pornography by child molesters on the Internet to lure children, resulted in passage of the 1996 Child Pornography Prevention Act. This law was struck down by the Supreme Court in 2002 but reinstated in limited form in 2003. Opponents of childhood pornography feel comforted that all fifty states have anti-child pornography laws on their books. How the Supreme Court will deal with these laws in the future remains to be seen. However, there can be no doubt that, on the whole, American society, regardless of liberalized attitudes in other areas of sexually explicit material, favors statutes protecting children from child pornography.

That's Entertainment!

Invention of the printing press by Johannes Gutenberg in the fifteenth century made possible the mass production of journals, religious tracts, books, and other writings. This resulted in a surge of censorship by those opposed to the doctrines preached and the opinions expressed. The works of Martin Luther, John Calvin, and Galileo were among the first printed works suppressed on the grounds that they violated the established religious beliefs of the period. At the same time, a widening distribution of erotic pamphlets and books aroused moral outrage and movements to suppress such material. The banning of writings judged immoral has often been followed by the censoring of views believed dangerous. With movies, it began with the regulation of films' moral excesses, but a probe of political content was not far behind.

Don't Go West, Young Girls

From the very first movies, religious and community groups in the United States were concerned with what they

MAE WEST DEFIED THE CENSORSHIP RULES IN MOVIES SUCH AS *GO WEST, YOUNG MAN*, BUT THE DAYS OF DIALOGUE STEEPED IN SEXUAL INNUENDO WERE SHORT-LIVED.

saw as loose moral values portrayed on the screen. Their concern was paralleled by the monitoring of another new invention—radio—where both language and subject matter were subject to government supervision. Subsequently, such supervision was extended to television, where the battle over what is suitable for public viewing continues to rage up to the present time, including such conflicts as Janet Jackson baring her breast in the middle of the 2004 Super Bowl and the sexually explicit action and language on cable television shows such as *Sex and the City* and *Deadwood*.

A series of scandals involving sex, drugs, and murder rocked the movie industry during the silent era of films before the 1920s. Some of this was reflected on the screen in material viewed as lewd and vulgar. Protests mounted from church and community groups. Chicago Cardinal Mundelein distributed a pamphlet entitled "The Danger of Hollywood: A Warning to Young Girls." In 1921, the United States Motion Picture Producers and Distributors of America hired former Comstock Law enforcer William H. Hays to clean up the industry and its product.

For the next decade, the Hays Office, as it came to be known, served as little more than a buffer to keep the government from imposing censorship on movies, doing little to really censor itself. That changed, though, in the 1930s, with the advent of gangster movies, the slinky sexiness of sirens like Jean Harlow, and the suggestive dialogue of Mae West. West's sensual, suggestive body movements and husky voice were too much for the morality of the times as she murmured lines such as "Is that a gun in your pocket or are you just glad to see me?!"

Dumping the Code

In 1934, the industry adopted a Production Code that was enforced in earnest. It dictated how long kisses could last, barred the speaking of such words as *virgin, pregnant,* and *syphilis,* banned nudity, prohibited married characters from sleeping in the same bed, monitored how much cleavage could be shown, insisted that sin be punished, and forbade profanity, No movie could be released without a "Seal of Approval." Strong influence had to be exerted to get a waiver from the industry censor to allow Clark Gable to say the word "damn" in the final scene of *Gone With the Wind.*

The rules held until 1953 when *The Moon Is Blue* was denied a Seal of Approval because it "dealt explicitly with the issue of virginity." Producer-director Otto Preminger released it anyway, and *Blue* was a big hit. By the late 1950s, the Production Code was a thing of the past. The films that followed fulfilled the pro-censorship forces' predictions, and in 1968 public outrage forced the industry to institute a rating system, which is still used. Both the effectiveness and standards of the rating system are currently questioned by those concerned with morality in film.

Movies with profane dialogue, frontal nudity, and simulated sex scenes are often shown on television, particularly cable television. Sometimes such matter is bleeped, or cut, but often it is not. TV Parental Guidelines have been set up by parents concerned about what their children watch. The ratings are shown at the start of all programs except sports and news shows. For parents who can't always monitor their children's viewing, a V-chip—built into most newer television sets—is available to read ratings electronically and block programs considered unsuitable for minors. The V-chip allows parents to control the level of ratings they want blocked. The television industry has set up a TV Parental Guidelines Monitoring Board to insure uniformity and consistency in establishing the ratings.

Withheld by War

Industry-imposed censorship of television and movies did not always have to do with sex and violence and profane language. Sometimes it had to do with politics. Sometimes it had to do with wartime morale.

Following the United States' entrance into World War II, right after the Japanese attack on Pearl Harbor, the classic 1930 film *All Quiet on the Western Front* was withdrawn from circulation. It was not shown again until after the war was over. The film dealt with World War I, and it delivered an anti-war message. The sergeant portrayed by Louis Wolheim tells his comrades-in-arms, "At the next war let all the Kaisers, Presidents and Generals and diplomats go into a big field and fight it out first among themselves. That will satisfy us and keep us at home." In its review of the film, *Variety* recommended that it be reproduced "in every language to be shown to every nation every year until the word war is taken out of the dictionaries."

We were losing World War II for almost the first two years after we entered it. Enlisting the support of the public was very important to the war effort. American boys were dying in far-away places. Their morale, and the morale of their families at home, might well have been undercut by the message of *All Quiet on the Western Front*. Those who oppose such justifications suggest that too often truth is the first casualty of war.

These conflicting viewpoints re-emerged in 2004 when Disney Studios refused to release *Fahrenheit 9/11*, a movie directed by Michael Moore that was highly critical of the Bush administration's handling of the 9/11 crisis and the subsequent war in Iraq.

This self-censorship led to an enormous public outcry. The film soon found other backers and broke all profit records for a documentary film. Nevertheless, many people

The Motion Picture Rating System

In 1968, the Motion Picture Association of America and the National Association of Theatre Owners established a voluntary rating system, still used today, to help parents judge which movies they want or don't want their children to see. The ratings, and what they mean, are defined by the film industry Classification and Rating Administration as follows:

"G—General Audience. All ages admitted. This signifies that the film rated contains nothing most parents will consider offensive for even their youngest children to see or hear. Nudity, sex scenes, and scenes of drug use are absent; violence is minimal; snippets of dialogue may go beyond polite conversation but do not go beyond common everyday expressions.

"PG—Parental Guidance Suggested. Some material may not be suitable for children. This signifies that the film rated may contain some material parents might not like to expose to their young children—material that will clearly need to be examined or inquired about before children are allowed to attend the film. Explicit sex scenes and scenes of drug use are absent; nudity, if present, is seen only briefly, horror and violence do not exceed moderate levels.

"PG-13—Parents Strongly Cautioned. Some material may be inappropriate for children under thirteen. This signifies that the film rated may be inappropriate for pre-teens. Parents should be especially careful about letting their younger children attend. Rough or persistent violence is absent; sexually oriented nudity is generally absent; some scenes of drug use may be seen; one use of the harsher sexually derived words may be heard.

"R—Restricted. Children under seventeen must be accompanied by a parent or adult guardian (age varies in some locations). This signifies that the rating board has concluded that the film rated contains some adult material. Parents are urged to learn more about the film before taking their children to see it. An R may be assigned due to, among other things, a film's use of language, theme, violence, sex or portrayal of drug use.

"NC-17—No One 17 and Under Admitted. This signifies that the rating board believes that most American parents would feel that the film is patently adult and that children age seventeen and under should not be admitted to it. The film may contain explicit sex scenes, an accumulation of sexually oriented language, or scenes of excessive violence. The NC-17 designation does not, however, signify that the rated film is obscene or pornographic."

Unrated films, movies formerly rated X, and pornographic films generally, are not considered by this system. Queries and concerns by parents will be answered promptly by the Classification and Rating Administration.

TV Parental Guidelines

Emulating the motion picture companies, the television industry created the following TV Parental Guidelines, which may be used with or without a filtering V-chip, to help parents monitor their children's viewing:

"TV-Y—All Children. This program is designed to be appropriate for all children. Whether animated or live action, the themes and elements in this program are specifically designed for a very young audience, including children from ages two to six. This program is not expected to frighten younger children.

"TV-Y7—Directed to older children. This program is designed for children age seven and above. It may be more appropriate for children who have acquired the developmental skills needed to distinguish between make-believe and reality. Themes and elements in this program may include mild fantasy violence or comedic violence, or may frighten children under the age of seven. Therefore, parents may wish to consider the suitability of this program for their very young children.

"TV-Y7-FV—Directed to Older Children—Fantasy Violence. For those programs where fantasy violence may be more intense or more combative than other programs in this category, such programs will be designated TV-Y7-FV.

"TV-G -General Audience. Most parents would find this program suitable for all ages. Although this rating does not signify a program designed specifically for children, most parents may let younger children watch this program unattended. It contains little or no violence, no strong language and little or no sexual dialogue or situations.

"TV-PG—Parental Guidance Suggested. This program contains material that parents may find unsuitable for younger children. Many parents may want to watch it with their younger children. The theme itself may call for parental guidance and/or the program contains one or more of the following: moderate violence (V), some sexual situations (S), infrequent coarse language (L), or some suggestive dialogue (D).

"TV-14—Parents Strongly Cautioned. This program contains some material that many parents would find unsuitable for children under fourteen years of age. Parents are strongly urged to exercise greater care in monitoring this program and are cautioned against letting children under the age of fourteen watch unattended. This program contains one or more of the following: intense violence (V), intense sexual situations (S), strong coarse language (L), or intensely suggestive dialogue (D).

"TV-MA—Mature Audience Only. This program is specifically designed to be viewed by adults and therefore may be unsuitable for children under 17. This program contains one or more of the following: graphic violence (V), explicit sexual activity (S), or crude indecent language (L)."

were harshly critical of the movie and felt that Moore misrepresented the administration and helped to undermine the war effort. It was not nominated for any Academy Awards in 2005, which many saw as a political statement.

The House Un-American Activities Committee

The most controversial examples of entertainment industry censorship occurred between 1947 and 1954. This was the beginning of the so-called Cold War, when fear of Communist infiltration into all walks of American life was at its highest level. In Hollywood it started with hearings by the House Un-American Activities Committee (HUAC) chaired by Congressman J. Parnell Thomas.

Thomas claimed that President Franklin Delano Roosevelt had encouraged Hollywood to make pro-Soviet films during the war. This was true in the case of *Mission to Moscow* (1943), when the Soviet Union was our ally and sacrificing millions of its citizens' lives in the war against Hitler. Aside from this, there was little evidence to support the charge. Thomas also contended that the Screen Writers' Guild was riddled with communists and other leftists. A major aim of the hearings was to show how these writers inserted subversive propaganda into movies. Sixty percent of those summoned to appear before the committee were screenwriters.

Ten of the screenwriters who were summoned—John Howard Lawson, Dalton Trumbo, Albert Maltz, Alvah Bessie, Samuel Ornitz, Herbert Biberman, Adrian Scott, Lester Cole, Edward Dmytryk, and Ring Lardner Jr.—refused to answer the key question asked by Thomas: "Are you now or have you ever been a member of the Communist Party?" They were prevented from reading statements claiming that the committee had no right under the Constitution to pry into their political affiliations since the

Communist Party was a legal entity under United States law. Pressed, they fell back on the Fifth Amendment, which forbids a person from being compelled to testify against himself or herself.

Soon after the writers took the Fifth, Hollywood studio executives announced that they had been suspended without pay. They issued a statement declaring "we will not knowingly employ a Communist." An industry-wide blacklist followed. The Hollywood Ten were subsequently convicted of contempt of Congress and served between six and twelve months in jail.

The Hollywood Ten have achieved the status of martyrs among liberals over the years. Some of them may indeed have been Communist Party members at some time in their lives. Others acted out of principle. Once a person admitted having been a communist, the committee would demand that he or she supply the names of others who had belonged to the party, or other organizations deemed subversive. Contributors to various causes, such as Russian War Relief during World War II, would be identified, as would others known as "fellow travelers." Fellow travelers were people who, while not members of the Communist Party, shared many of their beliefs and aims.

Today, more than fifty years later, the answer to the question of whether the Hollywood Ten were heroes or Communist propagandists depends on whether it is being asked from the political left or the political right. At the time, however, the Committee sought to prove its case by finding evidence of communist infiltration in the movies themselves.

J. Parnell Thomas and the HUAC committee attacked some of the most acclaimed films of the era as vehicles for communist propaganda. These included *Citizen Kane*, *Gentleman's Agreement*, *The Best Years of Our Lives*, *Crossfire*, and *The Grapes of Wrath*. A lesser film, *Margie*, was withdrawn from circulation in 1946 because of pressure from the committee.

Margie, starring Jeanne Crain, had been written by F. Hugh Herbert from a story by Ruth McKinney and Richard Bransten. It told the story of a 1920s high school girl whose bloomers keep falling to her ankles because of a faulty elastic waistband whenever she encounters the young male teacher who, by film's end, is her husband. A sub-plot concerns a high school debate in which the heroine criticizes the 1928 occupation of Nicaragua by U.S. Marines. The words "rank imperialism" are used to show why "we should take the Marines out of Nicaragua." They resembled Soviet accusations of U.S. Cold War policies.

HUAC censorship did not only affect movies that had already been made, and their writers. Through the industry blacklist, it destroyed the careers of directors, actors, film editors, and many others in Hollywood. Among them were Oscar-nominated Sam Jaffe; actor Lee Grant, who was also nominated for an Oscar and was cited for refusing to give information against her former husband; top star Larry Parks, who had portrayed Al Jolson in two movies; and character actor Lionel Stander, who testified that the only un-American people he knew of in Hollywood were members of the committee. Stander went on to become a successful Wall Street broker before returning to the stage, and eventually to the movies.

Red Channels and The Big Muddy

When HUAC chairman Thomas was convicted of embezzlement and sent to prison, where he encountered some of the Hollywood Ten, John S. Wood became the new head of the committee. Under his direction, a list of 324 suspected communists and fellow travelers was compiled. The names ended up on the industry's blacklist.

By this time, the content of movies was being screened carefully while the movies were made. The scripts were gone over by people like popular novelist and self-styled expert on communist propaganda Ayn Rand. A slew of anti-Communist movies were being produced to prove Hollywood's loyalty to American ideals. These included *The Red Menace* (1949), *I Married a Communist* (1949), *I Was a Communist for the FBI* (1951), and *My Son John* (1952). In *My Son John*, Helen Hayes learns that her son is a communist and turns him in to the FBI.

By now, the television industry was also reacting to the extreme anti-Communist temper of the times. In 1950, former FBI agent Theodore Kirkpatrick and TV producer Vincent Harnett began publishing *Red Channels*, a list of television writers, directors, and performers they claimed had been, or were now, members of subversive organizations. Free copies of *Red Channels* were sent to those who hired people in television. To get off the *Red Channels* blacklist, those accused had to voluntarily testify before the House Un-American Activities Committee. As in the movie industry hearings, to clear themselves they had to name names of others involved in left-wing causes. Among those listed in *Red Channels* were composer Leonard Bernstein, actor Lee J. Cobb of *Death of a Salesman* fame, actor John Garfield, playwright Arthur Miller, poet and humorist Dorothy Parker, and folksinger Pete Seeger.

Seeger was barred from television until 1968 when he made a guest appearance on the *Smothers Brothers Comedy Hour*. Tom and Dick Smothers's CBS program "was fueled by civil rights, gun control, and the peace movement." Seeger had long been active in speaking out and singing out against the war in Vietnam. For his appearance on the *Comedy Hour*, Seeger chose to sing *Waist Deep in the Big Muddy*, with its lyrics proclaiming that "Every time I hear the news/That old feeling comes back on/We're waist deep in the Big Muddy/And the damn fools keep yelling to push on." The song was understood by peace movement proponents to refer to those in high places who persisted in pursuing the Vietnam War. Following Seeger's performance, CBS took the *Smothers Brothers Comedy Hour* off the air—it was the last straw for an irreverent show that had consistently riled the network's self-censors. The questions raised by television networks and movie industry self-censorship, sometimes in response to government or other pressures, are the same today as in the 1940s and 1960s. Should communications organizations with such vast power to influence millions of people conform to some majority morality? When they don't, are they, as political science teacher David Lowenthal of Boston College claims, "running counter to the education of the young in schools, churches, and synagogues?" Does patriotism require that they filter out that which might be construed as anti-American propaganda? Should the rules be different in times of war, or terrorist attacks? The running time of movies, and the air-time of TV programs, is limited. Someone must decide what appears on both the big and the little screen. Even news stories must be weighed one against the other. Where does professional decision-making leave off and censorship begin? How shall it be decided what viewers—including children and young adults—should and should not be allowed to see and hear?

5

The Rules of War

United States government censorship has often clashed with First Amendment guarantees of free speech and freedom of the press. The First Amendment was written in the late 1780s as protection, in part, against government censorship. Still, U.S. leaders have periodically claimed that national security requires information to be classified, documents kept secret, and data withheld from the public. The safety of citizens, the protection of property, the avoidance of conflict, the need for frank discussion by policymakers not subject to criticism before decisions are reached—these and other factors are cited as reasons for restricting First Amendment rights.

War gives these factors added weight, and changes the rules of government censorship. For instance, it tips the balance in favor of national security over freedom of information. The war against terrorism and the war in Iraq created justification for new rules of government secrecy, military restraints on press coverage, and even curtailing

In times of war, the U.S. government has often imposed limits on freedom of speech. Here, a guard keeps watch over detainees at the U.S. Naval Base, Guantanamo Bay, Cuba, July 28, 2004. A war crimes tribunal to discover how prisoners were treated was soon to begin; a scandal led to the press unearthing possible torture of prisoners held there.

private citizens' freedom of speech. According to former White House spokesman Ari Fleisher, the 9/11 terrorist attacks "are reminders to all Americans that they need to watch what they say, watch what they do, and that this is not a time for remarks" that might affect the nation's resolve to fight terrorism.

A Delicate Balance

Advocates of free speech such as Nancy Chang, senior litigation attorney for the Center for Constitutional Rights, fear that too strict wartime censorship could result in making "legitimate political dissent" illegal. Such dissent—anti-administration, or anti-war—is based on the free flow of information, including accurate coverage of American troops in battle and civilian bombing casualties. Present military regulations governing the press in war zones severely limit reporters' ability to gather news, critics say.

Armed service commanders believe that such limitations are justified in an age when satellite television and Internet reports can be monitored by the enemy. A battlefield "scoop" can give away important information about troop movements, casualties, or tactics. The news conveyed to the public from the battlefield may put our troops at risk. As one retired army colonel observed, "It's the people's right to know versus the soldier's right to live." The Defense Department believes it can maintain a just balance between those two rights. Victoria Clarke, then Assistant Secretary of Defense for Public Affairs, acknowledges that "we have a significant responsibility to provide your correspondents the opportunity to cover the war. . . . Keeping in mind our desire to protect operational security and the safety of men and women in uniform we intend to provide maximum media coverage with minimal delay and hassle." Journalists who covered the U.S. military in Afghanistan believed that the government did not keep those promises. They formed the organization Military Reporters and Editors (MRE) to combat increased restrictions to battlefield reporting. "We've seen numerous cases where the Pentagon has restricted our ability to report on the soldiers, sailors, airmen and Marines who serve the people of this nation," according to MRE president James G. Wright of the *Seattle Post Intelligencer*. In Iraq, much of the information was handfed to reporters. living in safe zones, who did not speak the language, and had to rely on government flacks.

Historical Precedents

There is nothing new about wartime conflicts between the press and the military. During the Civil War, General William Tecumseh Sherman charged war correspondents with "inciting jealousy and discontent and doing infinite mischief." When Union General George Meade was the subject of criticism in a dispatch by Edward Crapsey of the *Philadelphia Inquirer,* he had the reporter tied atop a beat-up old horse facing the tail, hung a sign around Crapsey's neck that read "Libeler of the Press," and paraded him past his assembled troops.

During World War I, correspondents had to swear to a representative of the Department of War that they would not write anything that might give comfort to the enemy. They were subject to strict oversight by General John J. "Black Jack" Pershing, head of U.S. forces in Europe. The rules restricted reporting to stories based on handouts from army headquarters. When war correspondent Westbrook Pegler wrote a story about American soldiers dying in large numbers from pneumonia and smuggled it out to be telegraphed through London, British censors intercepted it and contacted General Pershing. The general killed the story and succeeded in having Pegler recalled to New York.

When World War II General Douglas MacArthur was the subject of articles critical of his politics by John Mc-Carten in the *American Mercury* and Walter Lucas in *Harper's* magazine, the pieces were suppressed by the army's library service and withheld from soldiers on the grounds of "security." During the Vietnam War, wrote Alaska Senator Mike Gravel, "the elaborate secrecy precautions, the carefully contrived subterfuges, the precisely orchestrated press leaks, were intended not to deceive 'the other side,' but to keep the American public in the dark." A Center for Public Integrity report on the 1990 Gulf War noted media exaggerations based on military reports of the effects of smart bombs, Patriot missiles, and bombing missions, concluding that information was "restricted or manipulated not for national security purposes, but for political purposes." Similar criticisms were made regarding the military's manipulation of press coverage during the invasions of Grenada in 1983 and Panama in 1989, and now in Iraq.

At the Front

Following the Gulf War, the Pentagon promised media groups more direct access in future conflicts. There are complaints by correspondents that this didn't happen in Afghanistan. The *Columbia Journalism Review* reported that during the first three months of the Afghanistan campaign, U.S. journalists were denied access to American troops more than in any previous war. The presidents of a group of twenty news organizations issued a joint statement of concern "over the increasing restrictions by the United States government that limit news gathering and inhibit the free flow of information in the wake of the September attack . . . We believe that these restrictions pose dangers to American democracy and prevent American citizens from obtaining the information they need."

Secretary of Defense Donald Rumsfeld denied that the military restricted reporters' access to the front lines of the war in Afghanistan. Anyone who wanted to go could go," he said. It left unanswered the question of just how far journalists could go. A *Washington Post* reporter, attempting to penetrate an area of an Afghanistan war zone, was turned back when a United States soldier pointed a gun at him. *Toronto Star* correspondent Mitch Potter was kicked out of a U.S. base in Afghanistan for reporting facts in violation of Pentagon rules. On December 6, 2001, when American troops were hit by a stray bomb near Kandahar, photojournalists were locked in a warehouse by Marines to make sure they didn't take pictures of the wounded servicemen.

One of the most controversial incidents of Afghanistan war censorship involved the July 1, 2002, bombing of a wedding party at a village in the province of Uruzgan by U.S. planes. Aircraft personnel may have misread the traditional shooting into the air of rifles by members of the wedding party as hostile action. In any case, the bombing killed 48 people and wounded 117 more. When news of it reached journalists in Kabul, many wanted to join U.S. military investigators flying there to investigate. Permission was withheld from all but two of the correspondents—a reporter from the U.S. armed-forces newspaper *Stars and Stripes,* and a cameraman from the Associated Press Television Network. Subsequently, restrictions were placed on the sharing of information gathered by the two correspondents. According to the *London Times*, UN investigators found that U.S. forces "arrived on the scene very quickly after the air strikes and 'cleaned the area,' removing evidence of shrapnel, bullets and traces of blood." The findings "pointed to an American cover-up." The commander of coalition forces in Afghanistan, U.S. Lieutenant General Dan McNeill, denied that his press officers stonewalled reporters so that coverage of the bombing would be held to a minimum.

On and Off the Air

Wartime government censorship is not limited to coverage of war zones during this time of terrorist threats. Instant technology, capable of carrying speech and images around the world in a matter of seconds, renders enemy propaganda a potent weapon in the eyes of the U.S. military, and increases the threat of revealing strategic plans and transmitting espionage information. Because of this, new restraints on free speech were proposed by the government in October 2001 after U.S. television networks broadcast two videos received from the Arab news channel, *Al Jazeera*. The videos featured urgings by Osama bin Laden and his top officers for Muslims to target U.S. citizens and institutions around the world. Following their broadcast, then-U.S. National Security Advisor Condoleezza Rice arranged a conference call with executives of the five major U.S. television networks.

Rice expressed the government's concerns. The tapes could result in harm to Americans at home and abroad. *Al Jazeera* coverage of civilian casualties due to U.S. bombings could undermine the support of our Muslim allies in the Middle East, and could weaken morale in the United States. The bin Laden tapes could have disguised coded messages for al Qaeda cells in America and abroad.

Some of the television network executives did not think there was a realistic danger of the *Al Jazeera* tapes transmitting secret messages. They could be dispersed much more easily, and widely, over the Internet. Nevertheless, the networks agreed to cooperate.

CNN promised to "consider guidance from appropriate authorities" when deciding what to broadcast. Fox News owner Rupert Murdoch vowed to do "whatever is our patriotic duty," in the realization that "a major diminution of civil liberties" was necessary because of "unpredictable but protracted terrorism within our borders." CBS president Andrew Hayward said it was "appropriate to explore new ways of fulfilling our responsibilities to the public."

Some believe that fear led the press to censor itself in Iraq. In the September 19, 2003, edition of *USA Today*, CNN's top war correspondent, Christiane Amanpour, said the press, intimidated by the Bush administration, failed to aggressively pursue stories. Of course, some in the media believed the self-censorship was warranted.

Fox newswoman Irena Briganti said, "Given the choice, it's better to be viewed as a foot soldier for Bush than a spokesman for al Qaeda."

In 2003, the U.S. military codified rules for the press that allowed them to travel with the military. They were given access to initial preparation when possible but were not allowed to give out specific information. If the agreement was violated, they would be asked to leave.

The Scientific Dilemma

Responsibility to the public has also raised censorship concerns in the scientific community. When the publication *Science* ran an article on the creation of a polio virus, the U.S. House of Representatives reacted. They called the report a "blueprint that could conceivably enable terrorists to inexpensively create human pathogens for release on the people of the United States." A resolution was introduced calling on scientists to "exercise restraint" before making such information "widely available."

Mark Frankel of the Program on Scientific Freedom, Responsibility and Law of the American Association for the Advancement of Science pointed out that circulating information to scientists while not "giving aid to the enemy," could not be done "without changing the fundamental way science is done and reported." This involves publishing the results of research in detail so that others may repeat processes and build on them. Ronald M. Atlas, president of the American Society for Microbiology said such restrictions might severely damage biomedical research.

The withholding of information did indeed hamper scientists investigating the anthrax threat that followed the terrorist attack of 9/11. The FBI ran the investigation while the Army tested suspected items for anthrax. The test results were top secret because of concern with national security. Key facts were kept from the public and the media. The Centers for Disease Control (CDC), the government agency whose job it is to protect the American public from disease, was barred from seeing the letters containing anthrax.

Because of this, the CDC had no way of knowing how easily the anthrax could become airborne and spread. Acting on the basis of what the FBI told them, the CDC informed the public that letters containing anthrax were only a danger to those who opened them. If CDC experts had examined the letters, it might have led to earlier closings of postal sorting facilities through which letters spiked with anthrax spores had passed, and job sites where employees were at risk. They would have detected factors, says Dr. Julie Gerberding, CDC's acting director for infectious diseases, which "affect the impact of the anthrax on humans."

The CDC was further hampered by not being informed that the anthrax was of a particular variety known as the Ames strain. This was a "weapons grade" anthrax produced only in United States military laboratories. The CDC was unaware that the Army had been manufacturing anthrax since 1992. Government peacetime censorship had also withheld this fact from the public because the United States had been producing anthrax in violation of the 1972 UN Convention on the Prohibition of Biological Weapons.

Viewpoints

"Any credible story that covers the impact of the Homeland Security bill should tell the public that they will not have access to vital information about the public's health and safety."
—Lucy A. Dalglish, Executive Director of the Reporters Committee for Freedom of the Press

"To those who scare peace-loving people with phantoms of lost liberty, my message is this: Your tactics only aid terrorists, for they erode our national unity and diminish our resolve. They give ammunition to America's enemies and pause to America's friends."
—former Attorney General John Ashcroft

"They plan to fight the war and then tell the press and the public how it turned out afterwards."
—CNN correspondent Jamie McIntyre

"Sometimes the truth is so precious it must be accompanied by a bodyguard of lies."
—Secretary of Defense Donald Rumsfeld quoting Winston Churchill

"We Americans are now the only people in the whole developed world who can't actually hear what our enemy is saying about us."
—New York University Media Professor Mark Crispin Miller

"I don't like censorship any more than anyone else, but if we don't have some kind of formalized censorship policy in effect. . . . I'm afraid all we're going to get . . . are briefings."
—*Nightline* anchor Ted Koppel

"The military has a very important reason for controlling information during wartime: Officials rightly worry that news stories will inform the enemy about troop movements or military plans, thus endangering U.S. soldiers."

—*Detroit Free Press* columnist Mike Wendland

"We have never done anything to endanger American troops or disrupt American military strategies. We simply haven't, and we never would."

—Retired chairman and CEO of CNN Tom Johnson

Lack of knowledge that the Ames strain was involved kept the CDC from making recommendations that might have saved the lives of two postal workers and three civilians. Marc Siegel, M.D., a physician working with a Senate committee inquiry, points out that "in the world of bioterrorism, the lives of innocent people depend on cooperation. FBI secrecy and domination is far too costly."

Government justification for producing anthrax is that threats of bioterrorism go back thirty years and more. It was necessary to cultivate anthrax if they were going to develop a vaccine. Anthrax was needed to conduct decontamination studies. Military spokespersons point out that new bioterrorism weapons cannot be dealt with unless they are first replicated. Nor, they say, can this be done effectively in a public spotlight. They conclude that while secrecy and censorship may dismay First Amendment advocates, they may be necessary weapons in today's war against terrorism. It is not a conclusion with which First Amendment advocates agree.

6
Words and Deeds

Zealous cases for official censorship in various areas are made by both conservatives and liberals. These involve both speech—the spoken word—and actions which may be justified as symbolic speech. Sometimes they involve local, state, or federal government; sometimes they involve institutions such as colleges or universities; and sometimes they involve businesses.

Speaking Navajo

One such case, involving a fast-food drive-in restaurant, illustrates the differing viewpoints of free-speech issues. It began during the year 2000 when, according to R. D. Kidman, whose family owns the R. D.'s Drive-In next to a large Navajo reservation in Northern Arizona, there were complaints from workers and customers that some employees were insulting them in their native Navajo language. Some people "said they felt verbally abused and sexually harassed," said Kidman.

His owner-family responded by asking all employees to sign an agreement that they would speak only English.

The agreement told the employees that "if you feel unable to comply with this requirement, you may find another job." Four of the Navajo women employees refused to sign, left in protest, and filed a complaint with the federal Equal Employment Opportunity Commission. The Commission, together with the four Navajo women, sued the restaurant for violating a section of the federal 1964 Civil Rights Act that says employers may not prohibit their employees from speaking their native language on the job.

As legal costs mounted for the Kidman family, ProEnglish, a group based in Arlington, Virginia, came to their aid. ProEnglish is an organization that rallies support for having English declared the official language of the United States. In September 2002, the case was heard in federal court in Phoenix, Arizona. As yet it has not been resolved. In 2003, the Kidmans instituted a policy that Navajo customers may be served in Navajo, and that Navajo employees could converse in their native language at break times. However, until the case is resolved, proponents of free speech, and those who would put limitations on it, will continue to argue the issues raised by the Navajo case.

"A Clear and Present Danger"

The spoken word has been a tool of protest against the government since the United States was founded. Reformers and rabble-rousers, crusaders and hate-mongers, pacifists and communists—these and many other groups have relied on the shield of the First Amendment to protect their speech. However, it hasn't always worked. Some limitations were spelled out by Justice Oliver Wendell Holmes Jr. in 1919. The case, *Schenck* v. *United States,* involved a socialist who had opposed World War I in what Holmes called "impassioned language." In upholding Schenk's conviction, Holmes wrote as follows:

"The most stringent protection of free speech would

not protect a man in falsely shouting fire in a theater and causing a panic. The question is whether the words used are used . . . to create a clear and present danger."

A week later, on March 10, this yardstick was applied in the case of *Debs* v. *United States.* Eugene V. Debs had been the Socialist Party candidate for president in 1900, 1904, 1908, and 1912. He had been convicted of sedition under the 1917 Espionage Act. He had made speeches against the war, telling young men that "you need to know that you are fit for something better than slavery and cannon fodder." The Supreme Court confirmed Debs's conviction, and he went to prison. In 1920 Debs ran for president from prison and got almost a million votes, more than any other third-party candidate up to that time. In 1921, President Warren Harding pardoned him and he was released.

The Fight to Talk Dirty

"Eugene Debs with an act." That's how Nat Hentoff, the anti-censorship author of *Free Speech for Me—But Not for Thee,* describes the late 1960s stand-up comic Lenny Bruce. What Hentoff means is that Bruce's act, filled as it was with four-letter words, also had social value. At that time, according to the Supreme Court, for it to be judged obscene, it had to be "utterly without redeeming social value."

Bruce's problem was that many—if not all—of the fifty states had obscenity laws that conflicted with that definition. For that reason, he was often arrested and convicted and bogged down in an appeals process that continued even after his death. It was a testament to how much he offended people.

"What I want people to dig," Lenny Bruce said, "is the lie": denying things that everybody does but you're not supposed to talk about. "If you *do* them, you should be able to *say* the words." Today most of the curse words he used are spoken in movies, and sometimes aren't bleeped out on television. Some people are appalled at this; others shrug it off.

It wasn't just the profanity that got Bruce arrested. In his act he went out of his way to offend just about everybody. He deliberately used words to slur people's ethnicity, race, and religion. He made fun of Jackie Kennedy trying to avoid bullets during her husband's assassination. It was meant to be satire. Today he is imitated by a host of rising young comedians, most notably Andrew Dice Clay, whose comedy is farther to the right than Bruce's was to the left. Like Bruce's material, their acts are considered by many to be in bad taste.

The Free Speech Movement

At the same time that Lenny Bruce was flaunting profanity on the stages of night clubs and cabarets, student activists were returning to the University of California, Berkeley, after a summer of fighting for civil rights in the South. When the university administration forbade them to use the institution's facilities for their campaigns, protests arose. The resulting confrontation marked the beginning of the Free Speech Movement, led by Mario Savio, a charismatic speaker and writer who accused the "university bureaucracy" of acting "to suppress the students' political expression." Savio inspired protesters to take over the university's Administration Building, resulting in the arrest of more than 800 students, the largest mass arrest of students in U.S. history up to that time.

On February 7, 1991, Senator Robert C. Byrd of West Virginia described how the 1960s Free Speech Movement at Berkeley "deteriorated into demanding the right to openly use Anglo-Saxon profanity and common obscenities in campus publications, in class discourse or in public seminars and lectures." That was the start, in Byrd's opinion, of "the process" by which "our entire cultural discourse is, day by day, being vulgarized, cheapened, uglified, coarsened and tarnished." He pointed out that people who regularly use obscenities and profanities are so used to it that they don't realize that others "might object to such a vocabulary."

Organizations like Morality in Media, the Family Research Council, and Concerned Women for America would like to see the standards of decency, which they believe were broken down in the 1960s, rebuilt. In some cases, the courts have shown sympathy for that position. One case that attracted much attention involved Cecilia Lacks, a St. Louis public high school teacher.

Lacks had her eleventh grade students write and videotape short plays. Some of the results dealt with gang violence. They included profanity and offensive racial and ethnic language. When the school administration said this violated the student discipline code, Lacks protested that the code applied only to behavior by students toward others. The school board fired her and she sued for damages. After a jury awarded her $750,000 based on her First Amendment claims of free speech, the school board appealed the verdict to the Eighth Circuit Court of Appeals. The three-judge panel of the Court of Appeals reversed the decision. Lacks then appealed the case to the U.S. Supreme Court. It upheld the Court of Appeals ruling that "a school district does not violate the First Amendment when it disciplines a teacher for allowing students to use profanity repetitiously . . . in their written work."

The Flag-Burning Controversy

Under the First Amendment, not all protected speech is written or spoken. There is also so-called symbolic speech, which involves an action. The most controversial example of this is the burning of an American flag. Back in 1984, during the Republican National Convention, Gregory Lee Johnson doused an American flag with gasoline and set it on fire. Johnson was the leader of a political demonstration protesting the policies of the administration of President Ronald Reagan, and the actions of some Dallas-based corporations.

Johnson was arrested and charged with violating a Texas law against treating the flag disrespectfully. He was found guilty, sentenced to a year in jail and fined two thousand dollars. After a state court of appeals upheld the verdict, Johnson appealed to the Texas Court of Criminal Appeals and the guilty verdict was reversed. In 1989, the U.S. Supreme Court upheld the reversal on the grounds that flag burning was a form of protest speech protected by the First Amendment. Brennan, writing for the majority, wrote that by punishing flag-burners "we dilute the freedom that this cherished emblem represents."

There was public outrage at the decision. A U.S. Senate resolution reprimanding the Supreme Court passed by a vote of ninety-seven to three. One of the three, Gordon Humphrey, was a conservative Republican. He called the resolution "an exercise in silliness." Not long after, Congress passed the Flag Protection Act of 1989, which was designed to punish anyone who "knowingly mutilates, defaces, physically defiles, burns, maintains on the floor or ground, or tramples upon any U.S. flag." A year later the Supreme Court struck down the act on the grounds that it violated freedom of speech.

In 2000, a proposal to amend the Constitution so that Congress might enact flag protection laws failed by four votes in the Senate. The amendment was reintroduced in 2003, and passed. Supporters like Tommy Lasorda, general manager of the Los Angeles Dodgers, believe that one of the best ways we can teach our children "respect for God and Country . . . is by protecting our flag from physical desecration." Writing against the amendment, Charles Levendosky, editor of the *Casper* (Wyoming) *Star-Tribune* editorial page, warns that "a nation that uses force to compel unity and patriotism is a nation on its way to a dictatorship."

Should KKK Crosses Burn?

Depending on what's being burned, positions on symbolic speech may do an about-face. Many of those who support flag burning as a legitimate form of protest do not believe that the flaming crosses of the Ku Klux Klan should be permissible expression under the law. In a Virginia case that reached the Supreme Court in 2002, African-American Justice Clarence Thomas made an uncharacteristically emotional statement, pointing out that a burning cross "is unlike any symbol in our society. There's no other purpose to the cross, no communication, no particular message. It was intended to cause fear and to terrorize a population."

The U.S. Supreme Court was reviewing a Virginia law that banned cross-burning, which the Virginia supreme court had said was unconstitutional. In doing so, they had reversed guilty verdicts in two cases. In one, a Ku Klux Klansman had set afire a thirty-foot-high cross on public land visible to neighbors and to cars on a state highway. In the other, two men had burned a cross on property owned by one of them, but located twenty feet from the home of an African-American family. In throwing out the guilty verdicts, the Virginia court cited a 1992 U.S. Supreme Court decision striking down a Minnesota law that banned cross burning intended to alarm or intimidate people "on the basis of race, color, creed, religion, or gender."

You Be the Judge

The following are real-life cases in which free speech was the issue. How would you decide them? The actual court decisions are on page 88.

JANET JACKSON REACTS AFTER SINGER JUSTIN TIMBERLAKE RIPPED OFF ONE OF HER CHEST PLATES SO THAT HER BREAST WAS BARED DURING THE 2004 SUPER BOWL HALF-TIME. THIS CONTROVERSIAL EVENT LED TO SANCTIONS AGAINST THE TELEVISION NETWORK ON WHICH THE SKIT AIRED, AND SELF-CENSORSHIP BY ALL OF THE TELEVISION STATIONS.

1. During half-time at the 2004 Super Bowl, as part of a musical skit, one performer tore the other's shirt, exposing her breast. The performer and the network were severely sanctioned. Should they have been?

2. When New York City merchants complained about pedestrians blocking sidewalks to look at the work of street artists, police arrested those artists who had not obtained vendor licenses. Pointing to sidewalk merchants who were allowed to sell books without a license, the artists said their First Amendment rights were being violated. Were they right?

3. A San Francisco clergyman who served on the city's Human Rights Commission quoted the Bible to reporters and on television, criticizing gay men as sinners against God. Removed by the mayor from the commission because of his outspokenness, the minister sued in federal court on the grounds that the First Amend-

ment guaranteed his right to express his views. Was his speech protected by the Constitution?

4. The annual St. Patrick's Day parade in Boston was cancelled in order to avoid having to march with gay and lesbian groups. Soon after, the anti-gay Nationalist Movement applied for a permit to march down the parade route. The city denied the permit, citing concerns about congestion, violence, and safety. The decision was appealed to a federal court. How should it have decided?

5. A pro-life group bought advertising space for anti-abortion measures in transit stations in Washington, D.C., Philadelphia, and Baltimore. The posters claimed that women who had abortions increased their risk of getting fatal breast cancer. When a federal health official complained that the advertisement was misleading and raised fears not backed up by scientific research, the area's Transportation Authority had the posters taken down. The advertisers went to federal court, claiming a constitutional right to express their view. Did they have such a right?

6. After Attorney Kevin Hendrickson represented John Muldoon in a probate case and won, he allowed Muldoon to pay his fee in monthly installments over a two-year period. After eighteen months, Muldoon began picketing his office with a large sign which read "UNFAIR LEGAL FEES CHARGED." When Hendrickson took him to court, Muldoon claimed First Amendment rights. Did they apply in this case?

7. An insurance company sent letters to accident victims who were policy holders to discourage them from hiring a lawyer. A series of legal actions were taken against the company for improperly giving legal advice. The company claimed it was acting well within its First Amendment rights. Was it?

You Be The Judge (Decisions)

Following are the actual decisions reached in the cases on pages 86 and 87:

1. The network and the performer were fined and sanctioned. As a result, television stations have greatly increased self-censorship.

2. A federal court decided that licensing street artists was unconstitutional and the U.S. Supreme Court upheld the ruling.

3. A federal court found that the clergyman's free speech rights did not extend to assuring him job security when he expressed anti-gay views while serving on a commission engaged in furthering human rights.

4. A federal judge said the free speech rights of those who wanted to parade had been denied. He struck down the city's parade permit law on the grounds that it provided too much power to ban marches. The judge also concluded that the city's real objection to the march had been the content of the message the anti-gay group was trying to convey.

5. The pro-life group's free speech rights were confirmed by a federal court on the grounds that advertising space in transit stations is a public forum and may not be censored. The U.S. Supreme Court upheld the ruling.

6. Muldoon lost. Circuit Court Judge Cynthia Cox ruled that "picketing for an unlawful purpose is not protected speech," adding that "this is not an issue of freedom of speech."

7. Several states decided against the insurance company. In West Virginia it was ruled that the flier violated state law against "unauthorized legal practice." A Connecticut court said it was illegal to discourage people from retaining an attorney. Pennsylvania found the company had violated unfair trade and consumer protection laws. New York fined the company. These and other states did not buy the First Amendment defense.

In the present case, Justice John Paul Stevens was concerned that the cross burnings had only been prosecuted because they constituted obnoxious speech. Justice David H. Souter argued that "the cross has acquired a potency that is at least equal to that of a gun." In 2003, the Court agreed that the Virginia law was unconstitutional, a violation of First Amendment rights. Writing the Court's majority opinion, Justice Sandra Day O'Connor said states could not assume that cross-burning was always intended to threaten people. Associate Justice Thomas strongly dissented, saying that cross burning has an emotional meaning that goes well beyond free speech.

7

Around the World

*"Any advocacy of national, racial,
or religious hatred that constitutes
incitement to discrimination, hostility
or violence must be prohibited."*

—Article 20 of the United Nations' International
Covenant on Civil and Political Rights

The United States signed the above proclamation banning
hate speech. However, when the Council of Europe adopted
a measure in November 2002 that made it a crime to broadcast such material over the Internet, it conflicted with the
free speech guarantees in the U.S. Constitution. When
France tried to block French citizens from buying Nazi
souvenirs online through the American-based Internet
provider Yahoo, a judge ruled that Yahoo did not have to
block the site because U.S. Web sites are subject only to
American law. This was only one of the many examples of
the contradictions in international censorship.

Among the countries of the world, there is even less
consistency over what may be censored and what may not
than among U.S. local, state, and federal jurisdictions.
History, cultural differences, and religious beliefs have resulted in censorship laws and punishments for breaking
them that vary widely from country to country. Many of them
are very different from the statutes and penalties in the
United States.

THE UNITED STATES IS NOT THE ONLY GOVERNMENT THAT CENSORS
READING AND OTHER MATERIAL; IN FACT, THE NAZIS PUBLICLY BURNED
BOOKS CONSIDERED "UN-GERMAN."

Worldwide Internet Controls

Germany, renouncing its past role in the Holocaust, prohibits propaganda promoting "the precepts of the Nazi
regime" over the Internet. Spanish Internet sites are forbidden by law to disseminate bigotry, and access is blocked to
hate sites originating in other countries, including the
United States. The Austrian Prohibition Act outlaws actions on behalf of the Nazi Party and has prosecuted the
Nazi computer network information exchange, Thule-Net.
Sweden, Denmark, Norway, Italy, and the Czech Republic
have similar laws.

Because the laws are worded and interpreted differently, hate groups have moved from country to country in order to avoid being prosecuted. They have established a pattern of closing down and setting up new Internet transmitting operations. At first such groups were making short hops from France to Belgium, or Germany to Austria to Sweden. However, in the mid- to late-1990s, as the laws began being more strictly enforced throughout Europe, more and more such sites closed down and reopened in the United States, where hate speech is for the most part protected under the First Amendment. Today, out of 4,000 hate sites worldwide, some 2,500 originate in the United States.

Not all of the regulation of the Internet in other countries, however, is aimed at stemming the flow of international bigotry. Some of it is intended mainly to exert control over a nation's own citizens. According to *The New York Times*, "China has the most extensive Internet censorship in the world." In China people are forbidden to access sites that threaten the system of government. Chinese Internet users must register with the authorities. The Chinese Ministry of State Security maintains systems to monitor the content of e-mail messages. Senders and receivers are subject to arrest and/or imprisonment if the messages contain subject matter antagonistic to the government.

Saudi Arabia controls the Internet by diverting all communications to a central server that functions as a censor. India, Uzbekistan, and some other countries keep the cost of the Internet very high in order to limit the number of people who can use it. In Turkey, Cofkun Ak, who operated Superonline, an Internet service provider, was sentenced to forty months in prison for disseminating a Web site discussion on "Human Rights Violations in Turkey." North Korea bans e-mail, and allows only government computers to access the Internet.

Suppression and Punishment

Foreign countries also censor the press and other media. In Australia, a government tribunal found that the *Australian Financial Review* had committed an unlawful act by publishing an article suggesting that Palestinians could not be trusted in Mideast peace talks. Films, including Mexican director Arturo Ripstein's *Black Widow,* in which a priest reveals the secrets of the confessional, and Martin Scorsese's *Last Temptation of Christ* (1988), were kept from being released in Mexico when the government banned them at the request of the Catholic Church.

A case that attracted international attention was that of sixty-four-year-old Egyptian-American sociologist Eddin

THE THAI MUSLIM STUDENT ASSOCIATION IS SHOWN HERE IN FRONT OF THE GOVERNMENT HOUSE IN BANGKOK URGING THE PRIME MINISTER TO IMPOSE CENSORSHIP ON MEDIA COVERAGE OF THE 9/11 ATTACKS AGAINST THE UNITED STATES. THEY SAID THAT MEDIA COVERAGE HAD TAINTED THE IMAGE THE WORLD HAS OF ISLAM.

Ibrahim. The State Security Court of Egypt said that Ibrahim, a professor at American University in Cairo, had "intentionally propagated false statements and biased rumors concerning some internal affairs that could weaken the standing of the state." Ibrahim had charged that Egypt persecuted its Christian Coptic minority and mistreated human rights groups. He had been sentenced to seven years in jail. When the verdict was challenged, he was tried and convicted again. This second conviction was protested by U.S. President George W. Bush, who threatened to limit U.S. aid to Egypt. The guilty verdict was set aside, and Ibrahim is presently awaiting a third trial.

More than thirty reports by international human rights organizations confirm the suppression of literature distributed by the Church of Scientology in Germany. Reacting to government orders or recommendations and most recently to action by the Berlin Senate of Science, Research and Culture, libraries have refused to stock books on Scientology even when the material is offered as donations. By contrast, under German law, pornography is legal.

Legalized Pornography

Each culture looks and regulates pornography differently. Some nations have very strict standards. In others, such as Germany, Denmark, and Sweden, pornography is easily available and of little concern to the legal system. Only child pornography is illegal in all three countries.

Those who favor legalizing erotic material point to evidence that the purchase of such items has decreased considerably in these nations in the years since the laws were relaxed. They say it proves the wisdom of the couplet by Geoffrey Chaucer, which advises:

**"When something's difficult, or can't be had,
We crave and cry for it all day like mad."**

They point to studies indicating that sex crime and crimes against women decreased in Denmark, Sweden, and Germany following the legalization of sexually explicit materials. Opponents, however, claim that the change in laws did away with the criminalization of many sex acts and that this is what accounts for the statistical decrease. They also claim that there has been as much as a 200 percent growth in sexually transmitted diseases. Censorship, they insist, might have stemmed this tide. There is, however, no evidence of such a result in Saudi Arabia, Iran, and China, where the penalty for selling or distributing pornographic material is death.

A *Fatwa* for Salman Rushdie

The effectiveness of death as a penalty was recognized by much-censored playwright George Bernard Shaw. "Assassination," Shaw pointed out, "is the extreme form of censorship." Death is the sentence passed on writers in many Muslim countries, where blasphemy is punished by the issuing of a *fatwa*.

A *fatwa*—a sentence of death—may be issued by a high Muslim cleric, or by a panel of spiritual leaders. In modern times only fundamentalist Muslim leaders—a small minority of the world's approximately 1.75 billion Muslim population—have issued *fatwas*. The most famous was the *fatwa* issued by the Shi'ite Muslim leader of Iran, the late Ayatollah Ruhollah Khomeini, against the author Salmon Rushdie.

Rushdie, himself a Muslim, had written a novel called *The Satanic Verses* (1988), which satirized portions of the *Koran*, the holy book of the Muslim religion. It was offensive not just to fundamentalist Muslims, or to Shi'ite Muslims, but to many of the 83 percent of Muslims who belong to the Sunni sect. Most Muslims, however, did not support the Ayatollah Khomeini when he informed "the proud Muslim people of the world that the author of *The*

A *FATWA*, OR SENTENCE OF DEATH, HAS BEEN IN EFFECT AGAINST AUTHOR
SALMAN RUSHDIE SINCE **1988** FOR WRITING A NOVEL WHICH SATIRIZED PARTS
OF THE *KORAN*, THE HOLY BOOK OF ISLAM.

Satanic Verses book which is against Islam, the Prophet and the *Koran,* and all involved in its publication who were aware of its content are sentenced to death."

The *Satanic* Victims

Following the issuance of the *fatwa* against him on February 14, 1989, Rushdie began a period of hiding and flight that continues to the present. It has been a time marked by much violence related to the *fatwa.* On September 14, 1989, four bombs were planted outside British bookshops owned by Penguin Press, publishers of *The Satanic Verses.* On July 3, 1991, Ettore Capriolo, the sixty-one-year-old Italian translator of the book, was beaten up and attacked by an Iranian man with a knife in his Milan apartment. On July 12, 1991, the Japanese translator of the book, Hitoshi Igarashi, was stabbed to death in Tokyo. In 1993, Aziz Nesin, a Turkish newspaper publisher who had printed excerpts of *The Satanic Verses,* was attacked by an angry mob. That same year William Nygaard, the Norwegian publisher of the book, was shot four times in the back by an Islamic extremist.

On February 12, 1997, the fifteenth Khordad Foundation, an Iranian revolutionary group, raised the bounty for killing Rushdie to $2.5 million. In September 1997, after the Iranian government said it would take no action to threaten Rushdie's life, three Iranian clerics urged their Islamic followers to kill him anyway. In October, 160 members of the Iranian parliament announced that the *fatwa* was still in effect. Later in October the price on Rushdie's head was raised by another $300,000. On February 12, 2001, the twelfth anniversary of the *fatwa,* the death sentence for Rushdie was reconfirmed.

The *fatwa* against Rushdie is still in effect. His life continues to be in danger, but he continues to write. In 1990 he published a book of stories, in 1991 a children's novel, and in 1997 an adult novel called *The Moor's Last Sigh.*

Words and Death

Could censorship have prevented the deaths of 220 people in Kaduna, Nigeria, in November 2002? The controversy behind the riots that caused the deaths was holding the Miss World beauty pageant during the holy month of Ramadan. Reporting on the controversy, Isioma Daniel, a columnist for the Nigerian newspaper *This Day,* observed that many Muslims "thought it was immoral to bring 92 women to Nigeria and ask them to revel in vanity." Then she wrote the words which most observers agree incited the fatal riots: "What would Mohammad think? In all honesty, he would probably have chosen a wife from one of them."

Nigeria is a country with a long history of tension and violence between Christians and Muslims. Protests against the Miss World pageant had been heated. Many journalists not directly involved in the situation believe it was unprofessional and irresponsible of Daniel to have written so provocatively. They believe that she knowingly poured oil on the fires of religious outrage.

They do not, however, believe that justified mobs torching the offices of her newspaper, police arresting the editor, or the deputy governor of the Nigerian state of Zamfara issuing the *fatwa* which forced Isioma Daniel to flee for her life. As Leonard Pitts of the *Miami Herald* wrote, "the problem is not religion. It's extremism and intolerance, no matter what creed" is involved.

Fatwa Against Fanatics

Shortly after 9/11, Islamic scholar and writer Ziauddin Sardar addressed his fellow Muslims as follows:

"A *fatwa* is simply a legal opinion based on religious reasoning. It is the opinion of one individual and is binding only on the person who gives it. But since the Rushdie affair, it has come to be associated in the West solely with a death sentence. Now that Islam has become beset with the fatwa culture, it becomes necessary for moderate voices to issue their own fatwas.

"So, let me take the first step. To Muslims everywhere I issue this fatwa: any Muslim involved in the planning, financing, training, recruiting, support, or harboring of those who commit acts of indiscriminate violence against persons or the apparatus or infrastructure of states is guilty of terror. . . . It is the duty of every Muslim to spare no effort in hunting down, apprehending and bringing such criminals to justice.

"If you see something reprehensible, said the Prophet Muhammad, then change it with your hand; if you are not capable of that then use your tongue (speak out against it); and if you are not capable of that then detest it in your heart."

From time to time, Rushdie comes out of hiding, but he must continue to protect his whereabouts. On March 15, 2002, Air Canada barred Rushdie from flying on any of its carriers. The airline said the extra security his presence required would cause delays of up to three hours for other passengers.

Heretics or Heroes?

Rushdie is not the only writer living under the threat of a *fatwa*. World famous Egyptian author and Nobel Prize winner Naguib Mafouz was condemned to death by fundamentalist Muslim Sheikh Omar Abdul Rahmame for having "insulted Islam" in 1994. The eighty-year-old Mafouz subsequently survived a knife attack. However, in his case, the fatal censorship might be said to work. He no longer writes.

Taslima Nasrin, a physician and author, was also sentenced to death for "insulting Islam." Fanatic mobs demonstrated against her in her native land of Bangladesh, demanding that she be burned alive. She escaped, but remains in hiding.

The list goes on. It includes Nasr Abu Zaid, targeted for criticizing the text of the *Koran*. Younis Shaikh, M.D., was sentenced to death in 2001; he was acquitted and freed in 2004. Mahmoud Muhammed Talai, a Sudanese author, was hanged because his books were supposed to have created religious turmoil. Of those still facing death for not adhering to religious censorship, the most noteworthy is perhaps Tahmineh Milni, an Iranian filmmaker soon to go on trial for making *Nimeh-ye penham* (2001), a movie reflecting some of the miserable conditions under which Iranian women live.

In each case, the crime censored by a sentence of death was heresy. It is a crime that has also been punished fatally by the zealots of many other religions. In both Europe and the Americas, people have been burned at the stake, boiled in oil, hanged and beaten to death for maligning, or refusing to accept as gospel, the religion of those passing sentence on them. The *fatwa* is no more representative of the Muslim faith than the Inquisition is of the Roman Catholic religion, or the Holocaust is of Christianity.

8
Protecting the Young

Protection of the young is the purpose behind much of the censorship in the United States. When it is exercised by institutions such as schools, colleges, and universities, it falls into a category known as *in loco parentis*—acting with parental authority. This means that while a student is on the premises, the institution can and should act as a parent. Like a parent, the staff of the institution may act to safeguard the student, to protect other students from him or her, and to supervise conduct so as not to disrupt the educational process or to interfere with the learning of other students.

All public school personnel have this authority. Private schools may establish stricter rules that students must obey. Although *in loco parentis* is generally meant to apply to the supervision of minors, older students at colleges and universities may also be subject to arbitrary rules affecting their behavior and free speech rights. In all these situations, censorship plays a major part.

AMONG THE MOST COMMONLY BANNED BOOKS IN SCHOOL LIBRARIES IS *CATCHER IN THE RYE*, A NOVEL PUBLISHED IN 1945 BY J. D. SALINGER. IT DISCUSSES THE "PHONINESS" OF ADULTS.

Unfit to Read?

A common battleground for such censorship is the school library. Here, parents play along with school authorities exercising *in loco parentis*. The most frequent scenario is one in which the parent objects to material in a school library book that their child has seen or read. The parent demands that the book be removed. Teachers, the principal, other parents, and perhaps the school board become involved. Pro- and anti-censorship forces take sides. Sometimes the case ends up in court.

Usually the book at issue has to do with sex or morality. Sometimes it has to do with issues such as abortion or gay rights. Parents may object because the book contains obscene language. There may be words in the book which are insulting to a particular ethnic group, race, or religion. Whatever the reason, the arguments pro and con will be spirited.

The nature of the books that have been banned from one or another school library varies widely. Included are such classics as *Catcher in the Rye* by J. D. Salinger, *The Grapes of Wrath* by John Steinbeck, and *An American Tragedy* by Theodore Dreiser. Some of the works of popular modern authors such as Toni Morrison, Alice Walker, Ken Follett, and Isabel Allende have been banished by school authorities. In Conroe, Texas, the Young Adult sex education book *It's Perfectly Normal* was ordered removed from the shelves, and in Cromwell, Massachusetts, two Newbery Medal-winning titles of young adult books dealing with witchcraft were challenged by a group of parents who also wanted the school board to prohibit teachers from dressing up as witches for Halloween. The popular *Harry Potter* series—which deals with wizardry—has also come under attack in some school districts.

Reasons and Rebuttal

Those calling for such censorship are often dismissed as naive or overly zealous. However, when their reasons are examined, there may be more justification than is immediately apparent. The Cromwell parents who wanted the books on witchcraft kept from their children, for instance, had serious concerns about a cult called Wicca that promotes witchcraft and that they felt might incite young people to commit acts associated with witchcraft, although a basic precept of the sect is to "do no harm." If the parents had been right about the sect being violent, it follows that there might have been good reason for forbidding teachers, who are role models for their young students, to dress up as witches.

There may be legitimate concerns about derogatory labels for African Americans in Mark Twain's *Huckleberry Finn*, or Richard Wright's *Native Son*, both of which may be part of a school's reading curriculum, as well as on the school library shelves. Young Adult books like Phyllis Reynolds Naylor's *Alice* series, which deals with adolescent sexuality, may confuse and upset third and fourth graders. In the aftermath of the Columbine school massacre and other in-school murders and violence, there has been understandable concern about school libraries offering non-fiction works about guns and hunting and military weapons, as well as volumes like *The Encyclopedia of Serial Killers* by Michael Newton, and novels with violent scenes, like the *Dune* series by Frank Herbert and *Artemis Fowl* by Eoin Colfer.

The right to censor school reading materials was upheld by the U.S. Supreme Court in *Board of Education* v. *Pico* (1982) when it decided that school boards "must be permitted to establish and apply their curriculum in such a way as to transmit community values . . . respect for authority and traditional values." The decision is supported by Steve McKinzie of Covenant Syndicate. "Parents who challenge the inclusion of a given text in a specific literature class and citizens who openly protest a library's collection development decision are only speaking out about things that they believe in," writes McKinzie. "We shouldn't be trying to ban free speech in the name of free speech. Let people speak out about what they care about, without being branded a censor or labeled a book burner."

Kerry Paul Altman, the parent of two children in the Fairfax County, Virginia, public schools, where censorship is an ongoing issue, disagrees. She believes that "forbidding our children access to literature that explores complex, if at times disturbing social realities is naive and potentially dangerous, as it does nothing to prepare them for the responsibilities and challenges of citizenship and community living. It is equivalent to sticking one's head in the sand and just about as effective."

The *Tinker* Clinker

In loco parentis has been interpreted in many public schools as justifying dress codes and speech codes. There is nothing new about dress codes. Not so long ago, male students in many public schools had to wear white shirts and ties to school, while female students had to wear skirts or dresses and were forbidden to wear slacks or jeans. During the 1960s and 1970s, most of these regulations were dropped. In the late 1990s, however, concerns were raised about high-priced sneakers and other expensive garments creating a divisive class system in some schools, mostly in the big cities, and causing fist fights and even more dangerous violence. As a result, a few schools devised inexpensive school uniforms and students were required to wear them unless their parents objected in writing. Most schools, however, followed a compromise procedure that banned obscene T-shirts, bare midriffs, designer jeans, and other items identified as provoking discipline problems.

The schools' right to censor students' clothing rests on the wording of the Supreme Court's decision in the 1969 case *Tinker v. Des Moines Independent School District.* The justices ruled that students wearing black armbands to protest the Vietnam War could not be forced to remove the arm bands by school officials. "It can hardly be argued," said the Court, "that either students or teachers shed their constitutional rights to freedom of speech or expression at the schoolhouse gate." However, the Court added this qualification: "Conduct by the student, in class or out of it, which for any reason . . . materially disrupts classwork or involves substantial disorder or invasion of the rights of others is, of course, not immunized by the constitutional guarantee of freedom of speech." In other words, the student who acts up may be legally slapped down as far as exercising First Amendment rights—whether oral or symbolic—is concerned.

Recently, school administrators have successfully relied on the *Tinker* exception. When fifteen-year-old high school sophomore Katie Sierra, of Sissonville, West Virginia, wore a T-shirt to school opposing the bombing of Afghanistan civilians, she was suspended. When she sued, a court found against her on the grounds that she had no right "to disrupt the educational process." She appealed the decision, but the West Virginia Supreme Court refused to consider her appeal.

Coke or Pepsi?

In a Van Wert, Ohio, case, high school senior Nicholas J. Boroff was sent home from school when he wore a Marilyn Manson T-shirt to class. Over the next four days, when he returned wearing a different Marilyn Manson T-shirt each day, he was forbidden to attend class. Boroff sued, but a three-judge panel of the Sixth U.S. Circuit Court of Appeals upheld a ruling against him, saying the school could ban the shirts because they were "vulgar, offensive and contrary to the educational mission of the school."

The *in loco parentis* function doesn't cover only speech and clothing. It has long since been decided by the courts that school personnel could search students' lockers for drugs. A recent Cleveland, Ohio, verdict determined that free speech rights didn't extend to the outside of students'

FREE SPEECH DOESN'T EXTEND VERY FAR FOR MINORS—SCHOOL OFFICIALS AND POLICE OFFICERS ARE FREE TO SEARCH STUDENTS' DORMITORY ROOMS AND LOCKERS IF THE PRESENCE OF DRUGS IS SUSPECTED.

lockers either—not even when the posters displayed there were meant to be patriotic. The poster, put up by sixteen-year-old Aaron Petitt, whose sister had been injured in the attack on the World Trade Center, showed bombers over Afghanistan with the message "May God have mercy, because we will not." Pettit was suspended for seven days, and the posters were taken down. Subsequently, U.S. District Court Judge Solomon Oliver decreed that Petitt must be allowed back in class, but stopped short of allowing the posters to be displayed. The school had said that students of Middle Eastern descent might be offended by them.

Not all such cases end up in court, and not all have unsatisfactory resolutions for the student involved. When "Coke Day" was celebrated at Greenbrier High School in Evans, Georgia, as part of the school's entry in a "Team Up With Coca Cola" contest, student Mike Cameron wore two shirts, one over the other. When the students, all wearing Coke shirts, positioned themselves to spell out COKE for a class picture, Mike Cameron took off his outer shirt, stuck out his chest, and displayed a Pepsi Cola shirt. For "being disruptive and trying to destroy the school picture," the school administration suspended him. The Pepsi Cola company, however, sent him a box of Pepsi shirts and hats.

Public School Speech Codes

Many public school districts have established speech codes in order to reduce conflict among students. In Howard County, Maryland, the school board established a policy prohibiting verbal and physical abuse based on "race, color, creed, religion, physical or mental disability, national origin, gender, or sexual orientation." Students who violate the rule receive counseling. Repeat violations may lead to suspension and expulsion.

A similar policy in St. Paul, Minnesota, also bans the

distribution of racially derogatory materials and pictures. The St. Paul policy includes teachers. It bars racial bias in instructional methods, placement of students, and books used in the curriculum. In Monroe County, Indiana, the speech code was enforced to discipline a student who called another pupil "an inappropriate name which could be construed as racist."

Backers of speech codes say they protect students against harassment, which can interfere with their ability to learn. Critics say they infringe on free speech rights. In Fairfax County, Virginia, the school board was caught between complaints that homosexual students were dropping out of school because of verbal insults, and parents who felt that an addition to the speech code meant to bar such language condoned homosexuality. In California, the state legislature reacted to protests by groups which included the ACLU, the California Teachers Association, and the state newspaper publishers association by overwhelmingly passing a bill requiring school districts to review the legality of speech codes barring taunts and slurs against certain groups, including Middle Eastern students.

Hassling at Harvard

The issue of speech codes has become particularly controversial on the campuses of colleges and universities where most students are over the age of eighteen and considered to be adults. Between two hundred and three hundred learning institutions in the United States have speech codes. To some extent, such measures have been restricted by law at public colleges and universities. Speech codes at the University of Michigan and the University of Wisconsin have been struck down by federal district courts. Private institutions, however, are exempt from such legal oversight.

A recent proposal to ban offensive speech at Harvard Law School was the result of a series of race-related incidents. The Black Law Students Association asked for the policy to combat frequent offensive behavior. They asked that a professor who had told his class that "feminism, Marxism, and the blacks have contributed nothing to tort law" be reprimanded. Many students and faculty members oppose the speech code measure, claiming that it infringes on campus free speech.

The invitation to a poet to speak at Harvard was canceled because he had made anti-Israeli remarks. When there were protests at the cancellation, he was re-invited. "This was a clear reaffirmation that the [English] department stood strongly by the First Amendment," said Harvard Professor Peter Sacks.

Speech Zone Systems

Yale University has long had a Use Policy which bans the "display of offensive, sexual material," but does not deal with speech. At Columbia University, the "Discrimination and Sexual Harassment Policy and Procedure" punishes "demeaning" speech to female students as sexual harassment. Brown University goes further with a sexual harassment policy that forbids "invitations, unwelcome verbal expressions, degrading language, jokes or innuendos, sounds or whistles," and "gestures." American University forbids "sexual humor," Cornell University calls "leering" sexual harassment, and the Dartmouth College policy states that "sexual harassment can be subtle and indirect, possibly even unintentional."

Some colleges and universities have sought a compromise in an effort to respect freedom of speech while forbidding hate speech. More than twenty institutions have established speech-zone systems that confine all forms of protests, demonstrations, and student speech to specific locations on campus. Anything may be said at these sites, but hate speech and other objectionable utterances are banned from the rest of the campus.

At the University of Houston, free speech zones were forbidden to amplify sound, or to carry signs on sticks. Students were required to register ten days in advance to hold minor protests. Such restrictions provide ammunition to those who oppose the compromise solution. An article in the *National Law Journal* finds it to be "a major threat to the ideal of free thought and free inquiry" because free expression "means freedom to choose where and when and to whom to speak, not just what to say."

The problem persists. Racist and anti-Semitic speech leads to violence on many college campuses. Muslim students are verbally harassed. Vulgar comments transform young women into sex objects. Free speech creates victims. On the other hand, restrictions on free speech diminish rights that citizens of the United States have always taken for granted. How should the conflict between the right to be free of verbal harassment and the right to be free to express oneself be resolved?

Afterword

Censorship is increasing in every area of American life today. So, too, are the reasons for it. The terrorist attack of 9/11, the war with Iraq, the presence of nuclear weapons in North Korea, threats of biochemical attacks, or nuclear strikes—all of these dangers and more have resulted in a tightening of national security precautions that includes policies of secrecy and the withholding of information from the general public. Secret trials, additional restrictions on the release of government documents, classified contingency plans for national emergencies—such measures may be necessary for the safety of our citizenry, but they may also be stretching the limits of our constitutional freedoms.

With the fear of terrorism, bias incidents toward Arab Americans have increased. These have surely been fueled by hate speech on campuses and off. Is such hate speech the equivalent of shouting "Fire!" in a crowded theater? Does it lead to violent acts? Is there a point at which such speech must be censored?

Production of pornography has grown tenfold over the last ten years. A 1998 study of the X-rated film industry by Forrester Research of Cambridge, Massachusetts, estimates revenues of $10 billion a year. In 2001, Vivid Entertainment, which produces erotic films for television and the Internet, grossed $1 billion in retail sales. Bill Asher, president of Vivid, points out that "we've gone from a market of hundreds of thousands to hundreds of millions."

Despite efforts to limit pornography, the national appetite for it has grown by leaps and bounds. The ability to view it in the privacy of one's own home has evidently opened the floodgates. Is this a response to a normal human appetite, or is it evidence of a moral decline in the United States? Is erotica an acceptable taste, and pornography unacceptable? When is the portrayal of a naked human body art, and when is it obscene?

Advances in technology have spurred action films for theaters and television that include an excess of graphic violence. Is there a valid difference between the violence of a fairy tale in which children are put in an oven and today's portrayals of high-tech mayhem? Do violent films lead to real-life violence? Are children who play brutal video games at risk of acting out what they see, as the Columbine High School killers did? Should the viewing of such games and such films be limited by parents? Should access to them by minors be limited by law? Shall we curb the manufacture of toy guns? Comic books which portray violence graphically? Cartoons on television?

In every area, when it come to censorship, the key question is who shall decide what should be censored, and what should not. Who shall decide for the government? Who shall decide for the children? Who shall decide for minorities? Who shall decide for adults who are offended by pornography, and for adults who choose to watch it? Who is to decide which is indecent, and which is adult entertainment?

Notes

Chapter 1
p. 11, American Library Association, Statement on Internet Filtering, July 1,1997.
www.ifla.org/faife/ifstat/alafilt.htm
p. 12, par. 1, Jason Krause. "Can Anyone Stop Internet Porn?" from *The ABA Journal*, 88, no. 9, September 2002.
citation.asp?tb=1&_ug=dbs+7+In+en%2Dus+sid+3CFCB 5ED%2D3BF1%2D4546%2DAF6410/23/02
p. 12, par. 2, Krause.
p. 12, par. 3, Krause.
p. 13, Author unknown. "Illegal Pornography is Illegal," from *Reefs and Rocks, Enough is Enough*, November 12, 2002.
www.enough.org/reefs.htm
p. 14, par. 3, Gina Hagedorn. *The Child Pornography Prevention Act Cannot Punish for Lewd Thought*, from *The Internet Law Journal* (updated September 2002).
www.internetlawjournal.com/content/ litigationheadline09010201.htm
p. 15, par. 1, Krause.

p. 15, par. 2, Krause.

p. 17, par. 1 Eric Blom. "Danger online: The Internet and child pornography," from *The Portland Press Herald,* October 11, 1998.
www.portland.com/specialrpts/danger/danger.htm

p. 17, par. 2,
www.sfgate.com/egibin/article.cgi?f=/c/a2003/06/04/MN144952DT2

p. 17, par. 3, Jane Hughes. "Sex offender jailed for Net 'seduction'," from BBC News, April 7, 1999.
news.bbc.co.uk/1/hi/uk/313299,stm

p. 17, par. 4, Peter Slavin. "How Safe Are Our Children on the Internet?" from the Child Welfare League of America, January 2002.
www.cwla.org/artisles/cv0201safeinternet.htm

p. 17, par. 4, Ibid.

pp. 18–19, "NRC Calls for Balance on Kids and Internet Porn," from *American Libraries* magazine, June/July 2002, Vol. 33, Issue 6, p. 22.

p. 20, par. 1, Slavin.

p. 20, par. 1, *Child Online Protection Act (COPA)—Overview,* Center for Democracy & Technology, November 14, 2002.
www.cdt.org/speech/copa/

p. 21, par. 1, Krause.

p. 21, par. 3, School and Libraries Universal Service Fund E-rate Fact Sheet.
www.ed.gov/Technology/eratefacts.html

p. 22, par.1, Linda Chavez. "Remember when libraries were for expanding the mind!?" *Jewish World Review,* Dec. 2, 1998.
www.jewishworldreview.com/cols/chaves120298.asp

p. 22, par. 2, FFL (Funds for Learning) Presentation on HR543, Children's Internet Protection Act, Nov. 13, 2002.
www.fflibraries.org/
Speeches Editorials PapersFFLHR543ResponseNumberTwo.htm

p. 22, par. 2, Tanya L. Green, J. D. "Predators in Your Neighborhood: American Library Association opens

door to sex crimes," Concerned Women for America,
Aug. 17, 2000.
www.cwfa.org/library/pornography/2000-08-17_ala.shtml
p. 22, par. 3, Ibid.
p. 22, par. 4, Children's Internet Protection Act. Tech
News.com interview with Judith Krug.
discuss.washingtonpost.com/wp-srv/zforum/02/
washtech-policy060302.htm
p. 23, par. 1, *The Freedom to Read Statement* of the
American Library Association and the Association of
American Publishers, July 12, 2000.
www.ala.org/alaorg/oif/freeread.html
p. 23, par. 2, *Encyclopaedia Britannica*, vol. 10 (Chicago:
Encyclopaedia Britannica, Inc., 1984).
p. 24, par. 2, Editorial in *The San Jose Mercury News,*
June 5, 2002.
www.bayarea.com/mld/mercurynews
p. 24, par. 3, Howard Berkowitz for the Anti-Defamation
League on *Hate on the Internet* before the Senate
Committee on the Judiciary, Sept. 14, 1999.
www.senate.gov/-judiciary/91499ad.htm
p. 25, par. 2, Ibid.
p. 26, par. 1, Pamela Mandels. "Rights Group Develops
'Hate' Filter," from *The New York Times* on the Web,
November 11, 1998.
www.nytimes.com/library/tech/98/11/cyber/articles/12filter.html
p. 26, par. 2, *Censorship vs. Freedom of Speech; The Case
of Hate Speech on the Net.*
mainline.brynmawr.edu/
-ccongdon/cs110spring98/Webpapers/hussain.html
p. 26, par. 3, Mandels.

Chapter 2
p. 28, par. 1, *Encyclopaedia Britannica,* vol. 3 *(Chicago:*
Encyclopaedia Britannica Inc., 1984).
p. 28, par. 3, G. L. Simons. *Simons Book of World Sexual
Records* (New York: Amjon Publisher Inc., 1976).
p. 29, par. 1, Simons.

p. 29, par. 2, Ova Brusendorff and Poul Henningsen. *Love's Picture Book: Vol. IV, The History of Pleasure and Moral Indignation*, trans. Elsa Gress (New York: Lyle Stuart, 1969).

p. 29, pars. 5, 6, *Encyclopaedia Britannica*, vol. VII.

p. 30, par. 2, Divorce Statistics Collection from Americans for Divorce Reform.
www.divorcereform.org/rates.html

p. 30, par. 3, "National Right To Life applauds sustained drop in U.S. Abortion Rate" (Centers for Disease Control statistics) from National Right to Life.
www.nrlc.org/press_releases_new/abortionratedrop.htm

p. 30, par. 4, Cheryl Wetzstein. "Out of Wedlock Births Soar," from National Center for Policy Analysis and *Washington Times*, Nov. 9, 1999.
www.ncpa.org/pd/social/pd110999c.html

p. 30, par. 5, Cheryl Wetzstein. "Teen Birthrates Here Still Higher Than in Some Other Major Countries," from National Center for Policy Analysis and *Washington Times*, Nov. 29, 2001.
www.ncpa.org/iss/soc/pd112901b.html

p. 30, par. 6, "Sexual Diseases and Births Among Unwed Teens," from National Center for Policy Analysis and *Congressional Quarterly*, July 10, 1998.
www.ncpa.org/pd/social/spjul98c.html

p. 31, par. 1, Johnathon Allen. "The Tragedy of Teen Suicide," from *Teenagers Today*.
teenagerstoday.com/resources/articles/teensuicide.htm

p. 31, par. 2, Joyesha Chesnick. "Society Slow to Believe It's Happening," *Tucson Citizen*, Oct. 14, 2002.
www.tusconcitizen.com/local/archive/02/molest/10 14 02molest side1.html

p. 31, par. 3, Sexual Assault Statistics from *Men Against Sexual Assault*. (Compilation: 1996–2000).
sa.rochester.edu/masa/stats.html

p. 33, par. 1, Carl Sifakis. *The Encyclopedia of American Crime* (New York: Facts on File, 1982).

p. 33, par. 1, Ibid.

p. 33, par. 2, Patricia Schroeder. "Comstock Act Still On The Books" (speech in the House of Representatives, Sept. 24, 1996). www.arentfox.com/quickGuide/businessLines/telemed/ehealtht...schroeder.92496.htm

p. 33, par. 3, Schroeder.

p. 34, par. 3, Susan Kullman Puz. "Victoria C. Woodhull: The First Woman to Run for President," from *Legal Contender*. www.class.csupomona.edu/his/skpuz/hst202/Woodhull/WQart.html

p. 36, par. 1, Sifakis.

p. 37, par. 2, Harry Reichenbach. *Phantom Fame*, quoted in *September Morn*. www.sniggle.net/septmorn.php

Chapter 3

p. 39, par. 1, Bill of Rights, Amendment X.

p. 39, par. 2, *Encyclopaedia Britannica*, vol. 10 (Chicago: Encyclopaedia Britannica Inc., 1984).

p. 41, par. 2, *Encyclopaedia Britannica*, vol. 3.

p. 41, par. 2, Edward deGrazia. *Girls Lean Back Everywhere: The Law of Obscenity and the Assault on Genius* (New York: Random House, 1992).

p. 42, par. 2, DeGrazia.

p. 42, par. 2, Elder Witt, ed. *The Supreme Court and Individual Rights* (Washington, DC: Congressional Quarterly Inc. 1980).

p. 43, par. 1, *Roth* v. *United States* (1957), Supreme Court of the United States, Case No. 582. www.bc.edu/bc_org/avp/cas/comm/free_speech/roth.html

p. 43, par. 2, Witt.

p. 44, par. 1, Bob Woodward and Scott Armstrong. *The Brethren: Inside the Supreme Court* (New York: Simon and Schuster, 1979).

p. 44, par. 2, Witt.

p. 44, par. 4, Woodward and Armstrong.

p. 45, par. 1, DeGrazia.

p. 45, par. 3, Witt.

pp. 46-47, Woodward and Armstrong.

p. 48, par. 2, Ted Gottfried. *Pornography: Debating the Issues* (Springfield, NJ: Enslow Publishers, Inc., 1997).

p. 49, pars. 1–3, *Summary of Laws Against Obscenity and Pornography* (New York: Morality in Media, 1995). Quoting *Commonwealth* v. *Sharpless* (Pennsylvania Supreme Court, 1815).

p. 49, par. 4, Witt.

p. 50, par. 1, Robin Morgan. *Going Too Far: The Personal Chronicle of a Feminist* (New York: Random House, 1977).

p. 50, par. 2, Nadine Strossen. *Defending Pornography* (New York: Scribner, 1995).

p. 50, par. 2, Andrea Dworkin and Catharine MacKinnon. *Pornography and Civil Rights: A New Day for Women's Equality* (Minneapolis: Organizing Against Pornography, 1988).

p. 50, par. 3, Strossen.

p. 51, par. 1, Strossen.

p. 51, par. 1, Strossen.

p. 51, par. 2, Strossen.

p. 52, par. 2, DeGrazia.

Chapter 4

p. 55, par. 2, Kenneth Anger. *Hollywood Babylon* (New York: Dell Paperbacks, 1981).

p. 55, par. 3, Leta W. Clark. *Women, Women, Women: Quips, Quotes and Commentary* (New York: Drake Publishers Inc., 1977).

p. 56, par. 2, Leslie Halliwell. *Halliwell's Film Guide*, 6th Edition (New York: Scribner, 1987).

p. 57, par. 2, Jon Weiner. "Quiet in Hollywood," *The Nation*, Dec. 9, 2002.

pp. 58–59, "Reasons for Movie Ratings (CARA)— Frequently Asked Questions" www.filmratings.com/questions.htm

pp. 60-61, "Understanding the TV Ratings"

www.tvguidelines.org/ratings.asp

p. 62, par. 1, Frank Rich. *The New York Times*, May 23, 2004. nytimes.com/2004/04/23/arts/23RICH.html?ei=500&en8 1516ec141284fba&ex=1400644800&partner=USERLA

p. 62, par. 4, Lester Cole. *Hollywood Red* (Palo Alto, CA: Ramparts Press, 1981).

p. 64, par. 1, Dialogue from the movie *Margie*, scripted by F. Hugh Herbert.

p. 65, par. 2, Frazier Moore. "Revisiting the '60s and the Smothers Brothers fight to laugh about it," the *Miami Herald*, Dec. 3, 2002.

p. 66, par. 1, Pete Seeger. "Waist Deep in the Big Muddy," *Gaughan's Song Archive*. www.dickalba.demon.co.uk/songs/texts/bigmuddy.html

p. 66, par. 2, David Lowenthal. "The Entertainment Industry Should Be Censored," *Censorship* (Opposing Viewpoints) (San Diego, CA: Greenhaven Press, Inc., 2002).

Chapter 5

p. 69, par. 1, Alan Pittman. "Censorship: Can a free press survive America's new war?" *Eugene Weekly*, Nov. 21, 2001. www.eugeneweekly.com/archive/11_21_01/ coverstory.html

p. 69, par. 1, Nancy Chang. "Silencing Political Dissent: How the USA PATRIOT Act Undermines the Constitution," from the Center for Constitutional Rights, March 2002. openmedia@sevenstories.com

p. 69, par. 2, J. B. "The Trouble With Censorship," *The Daily War Watch*, Nov. 3, 2001. www.democraticunderground.com/whopper/01/11/03_ censorship.html

p. 69, par. 2, Stephen Lee. "Media Access in War" from Newsaic, Jan. 28, 2002. www.newsaic.com/ftsvn127-06n.html

p. 70, par. 1, "Military Reporters Join Forces to Fight Access, Restrictions," from The Reporters Committee for Freedom of the Press, Oct. 23, 2002.

www.rcfp.org/news/2002/1023concer.html

p. 70, par. 1, slate.msn.com/id/2086110

p. 70, par. 1, R. S. Thorndike. *The Sherman Letters* (New York: unpublished, 1894).

p. 70, par. 1, Philip Knightley. *The First Casualty* (New York: Harcourt Brace Jovanovich, 1975).

p. 71, par. 1, William Manchester. *American Caesar* (Boston: Little, Brown and Company, 1978).

p. 71, par. 1, Senator Mike Gravel. Introduction to *The Pentagon Papers*, vol. 1 (Boston: Beacon Press, 1971).

p. 71, par. 1, Pittman.

p. 71, par. 2, Pittman.

p. 72, par. 1, William Walker. "Rumsfeld Charms the Media While Defending Censorship," *Toronto Star*, April 11, 2002.

p. 72, par. 2, "Pentagon Tried to Cover Up Wedding Massacre," *The Times of London*, July 29, 2002.

www.plp.org/misc/ftbraggbox0702.html

p. 74, par. 1, Pittman.

p. 74, par. 2, Julian Borger and Patrick Barkham. "Attack on Afghanistan: Media: US television to censor videos from Bin Laden: Networks agree limits on tapes from wanted terrorist leader," *The Guardian*, Oct. 12, 2001.

p. 74, par. 4, *USA Today*, Sept. 14, 2004.

p. 74, par. 5, Faith McLellan. "Academic Freedom or speaking with the enemy?" *Lancet*, Sept. 7, 2002.

p. 75, par. 2, McLellan.

p. 75, par. 3, Marc Siegel. "The Anthrax Fumble," *The Nation*, March 18, 2002.

p. 76, par. 1, "Reporters Committee Warns of Severe Restrictions in Homeland Security Bill," news release from The Reporters Committee for Freedom of the Press, Nov. 19, 2002.

www.rcfp.org/news/releases.view.cgi?2002_11_19_homeland.txt

p. 76, par. 2, Deirdre Shesgreen. "Ashcroft Accuses Critics of Helping Enemy; He Rejects Complaints About Justice Department Actions," *St. Louis Post-Dispatch*, Dec. 7, 2001.

p. 76, par. 3, Alan Pittman. "Censorship: Can a free press survive America's new war?" *Eugene Weekly*, Nov. 12, 2001. www.eugeneweekly.com/archive/11_21_01/coverstory.html

p. 76, par. 4, Ibid.

p. 76, par. 5, Ibid.

p. 76, par. 6, Brian Lambert. "Media: Koppel says war coverage will change," *Pioneer Press*, Sept. 21, 2002. www.twincities.com/mld/twincities/entertainment/columnists/brian_lambert/4118838.htm23.

p. 77, par. 1, Mike Wendland, "Censorship or National Security," *The New York Times Upfront*, Dec. 16, 2002. teacher.scholastic.com/upfront/issue7adebate.htm

p. 77, par. 2, Lambert.

p. 78, par. 2, Antonio Regaldo, Gary Fields, and Mark Schoofs. "FBI Makes Military Labs Key Focus on Anthrax," *The Wall Street Journal*, Feb. 12, 2002.

Chapter 6

p. 79, par. 2, Michael Janofsky. "Ban on Speaking Navajo Leads Café Staff to Sue," *The New York Times*, Jan. 20, 2002.

p. 79, par. 2, Ibid.

p. 80, par. 1, *Fortune* magazine. www.fortune.com/fortune

p. 80, par. 2, Elder Witt, ed. *The Supreme Court and Individual Rights* (Washington, DC: Congressional Quarterly Inc., 1980).

p. 80, par. 3, Oliver Wendell Holmes Jr. *Schenk* v. *United States*, in *Bartlett's Familiar Quotations*, 14th Edition (Boston: Little Brown and Company, 1968).

p. 81, par. 1, Witt.

p. 81, par. 2, Nat Hentoff. *Free Speech for Me—But Not for Thee* (New York: HarperCollins, 1992).

p. 81, par. 2, Witt.

p. 82, par. 2, Mario Savio. "An End to History," *Humanity*, December 1964.

www.fsm-a.org/stacks/endhistorysavio.html
p. 82, par. 3, Senator Robert C. Byrd. "The Dirty
Dictionary," The Congressional Record, Feb. 7, 1991.
www.senate.gov/~byrd/speech-dictionary.htm
p. 83, par. 2, Chip Rowe. "Free Speech or Not Free
Speech?" Playboy, August 1999.
www.chiprowe.com/articles/free-speech-quiz.html
p. 84, par. 2, Charles Levendosky. "Flag Desecration
Should Not Be Banned," Censorship (Opposing
Viewpoints) (San Diego, CA: Greenhaven Press, Inc., 2002).
p. 84, par. 3, "The Flag Desecration Amendment" from
The Freedom Forum. www.freedomforum.org/packages/
first/Flag/timeline.htm
p. 84, par. 3–p.85, par. 1, Tommy Lasorda. "Flag Desecration Should Be Banned," Censorship (Opposing View
points)(San Diego, CA: Greenhaven Press, Inc., 2002).
p. 85, par. 1, Levendosky.
p. 85, par. 2, Linda Greenhouse. "An Intense Attack By
Justice Thomas On Cross Burning," The New York
Times, Dec. 12, 2002.
p. 85, par. 3, Robert Marus. "Supreme Court will hear
cross-burning case," APB Washington Bureau, June 10,
2002.
www.baptiststandard.com/2002/6_10/pages/court.html
p. 87, par. 4, Rowe.
chiprowe.com/articles/free-speech-quiz.html
p. 88, par. 7, Rowe.
p. 88, par. 8, Rowe.
p. 89, par. 1, First Amendment Forum: "Supreme Court
debates whether cross burning is protected free speech,"
Associated Press and Post-Gazette.com.
www.post-gazette.com/FirstAmendment/20021211crossp5.asp
p. 89, par. 1, Reginald C. Oh. "Supreme Court Watch," in
The Section of State and Local Government Law,
American Bar Association Web site.
www.abanet.org/statelocal/lawnews/summer03/supreme
court.html (accessed January 25, 2005.)

Chapter 7

p. 91, par. 1, "Free Speech and the Global Information Infrastructure," A Regulatory Web. www.mttlr.org/volthree/foster_art.html

p. 92, par. 2, "China Has World's Tightest Internet Censorship," *The New York Times,* as quoted by the Clear Harmony Web site. clearharmony.net/cat/c1134/c1134.html

p. 92, par. 2, Kemal Altintas, Tolga Aydin, and Varol Akman, "Censoring the Internet: The Situation in Turkey," *firstmonday,* vol. 7, No. 6, June, 2002. www.firstmonday.dk/issues/issue7_6/altinta/

p. 92, par. 3, Ibid.

p. 93, par. 2, "New trial is ordered for Egyptian activist," *International Herald Tribune,* Dec. 14, 2002.

p. 94, par. 3, Geoffrey Chaucer. *The Canterbury Tales,* quoted in *Censoring Pornography Is Counterproductive* www.humanismbyjoe.com/Censoring_Porn.htm.

p. 95, par. 2, George Bernard Shaw. Part 1 of *The Rejected Statement* in *Bartlett's Familiar Quotations,* 14th Edition (Boston: Little Brown and Company, 1968).

p. 96, par. 2, Ayatollah Ruhollah Khomeini. *Fatwa* of February 1989 against Salman Rushdie from *Book Burning and Censorship.* www.rjgeib.com/thoughts/burning/sr-death.html

p. 98, par. 1, www.muktu_mona.com/news/shaikh_free.htm

p. 98, par. 3, Leonard Pitts. "Ungodly slaughter in God's name," *Miami Herald*, Nov. 30, 2002.

p. 99, Ziauddin Sardar. "My Fatwa on the Fanatics," *The Guardian*, Sept. 23, 2001. www.pass.to/newsletter/my_fatwa_against_the_fanatics.htm

p. 100, par. 1, Isioma Daniel. *ThisDay*, Nov. 16, 2002, quoted in *The Words That Triggered an Islamic Death Sentence* on The Memory Hole. thememoryhole.com/religion/miss-world.htm

p. 100, par. 2, Susan Stephan. "Intellectual Censorship in

Islam: A Matter of Life and Death." iranscope.ghand chi.com/Anthology/Islam/intelismal.htm
p. 100, par. 3, Stephan.

Chapter 8
p. 105, par. 1, Mychele B. Brickner. "School Book Bans: Sense or Censorship?" *Today: International Child and Youth Care Network*, Aug. 10, 2001. www.cyc-net.org/today/today010810.html
p. 105, par. 2, Steve McKinzie. "Banned Books Week 1997: A Case of Misrepresentation," *Covenant Syndicate*, vol. 1, no. 49. capo.org/opeds/banbook.html
p. 106, par. 1, Brickner.
p. 106, par. 3, *Constitutional Topic: Student Rights* from The United States Constitution Online, Jan. 2, 2003. www.usconstitution.net/consttop_stud.html
p. 107, par. 1, "Teen barred from forming anarchy club, wearing anti-war T-shirt," The Associated Press, Nov. 2, 2001. www.freedomforum.org/templates/document.asp? documentID=15289
p. 107, par. 2, "High Court refuses to hear Marilyn Manson T-shirt case," The Associated Press, March 20, 2001. www.freedomforum.org/templates/document.asp? docu mentID=13472
p. 109, par. 1, "School lessons in free expression send mixed messages," Freedom Forum, Jan. 2, 2003. www.freedomforum.org/templates/document.asp? documentID=15111
p. 109, par. 2, Michael Moore. *Stupid White Men* (New York: Regan Books of HarperCollins, 2001).
p. 109, par. 3, Peter Schmidt. "Speech Codes Tread Line Between Student Protection, First Amendment," *Education Week*, Dec. 2, 1992. www.edweek.org/ew/ewstory.cfm?slug=13speech.h12
p. 110, par. 1, Schmidt.

p. 111, par. 1, "Is Harvard Law getting touchy-feely?" CNN.com/Education, Nov. 24, 2002). www.cnn.com/2002/EDUCATION/11/24/harvard.speech.ap/

p. 111, par. 2, Ibid.

p. 111, par. 3, Jay Mathews. "The Betrayal of Free Expression on America's Campuses—A Sampling by the Foundation for Individual Rights in Education," *The Washington Post*, Nov. 10, 2002. www.thefire.org/offsite/data/washpost_111202.html

p. 112, par. 1, Harvey A. Silverglate, and Joshua Gewolb. "Muzzling free speech," from *The National Law Journal*, vol. 24, no. 54, Sept. 30, 2002. citation.asp?tb=1&_ug=dbs+7+In+en%2Dus+sid+3CFCB5ED %2D3BF1%2D4546%2DAF6410/23/02

Afterword

p. 114, par. 1, "San Fernando's Open Secret," CBSNEWS.com, Nov. 26, 2002. www.cbsnews.com/stories/2002/11/25/entertainment/ main530805.shtml

All Internet sites accessible as of Nov. 12, 2004, unless otherwise noted.

Further Information

Further Reading

Bode, Janet. *The Voices of Rape*. New York: Franklin Watts, 1990.

DeGrazia, Edward. *Girls Lean Back Everywhere: The Law of Obscenity and the Assault on Genius*. New York: Random House, 1992.

Ferguson, Donna. *The Assault on America's Children*. Newport Beach, CA: Harbor House West, 1994.

Gottfried, Ted. *The American Media*. New York: Franklin Watts, 1997.

Hull, Mare E. *Censorship in America*. Santa Barbara, CA: ABC-CLIO, 1999.

Murphy, J., and K. Tucker. *Stay Tuned: Raising Media-Savvy Kids in the Age of the Channel-Surfing Couch Potato*. New York: Doubleday, 1996.

Reisman, Judith A. *Kinsey: Crimes and Consequences*. Arlington, VA: The Institute for Media Education, 1998.

Roleff, Tamara L. ed., *Censorship*. (Opposing Viewpoints). San Diego, CA: Greenhaven Press, Inc., 2002.

Strossen, Nadine. *Defending Pornography*. New York: Scribner, 1995.

Zeinert, Karen. *Free Speech: From Newspapers to Music Lyrics*. Springfield, NJ: Enslow Publishers, Inc., 1995.

Organizations to Contact

American Civil Liberties Union (ACLU)
125 Broad Street, New York, NY 10004
Phone: (212) 549-2500
Fax: (212) 549-2646
www.aclu.org

American Library Association (ALA)
50 E. Huron St., Chicago, IL 60611
Phone: (800) 545-2433
Fax: (312) 440-9374
www.ala.org

Enough Is Enough
(Donna Rice Hughes, president)
746 Walker Road, Suite 116, Great Falls, VA 22066
www.enough.org
www.protectkids.com

Family Research Council (FRC)
700 13th St. NW, Suite 500, Washington, DC 20005
Phone (203) 393-2100
Fax: (202) 393-2134
www.frc.org

Free Speech Coalition
PO Box 10480, Canoga Park, CA 91309
Phone: (800) 845-8503 or (818) 348-9373
E-mail: freespeech@pacificnet.net
www.freespeechcoalition.com

Morality in Media (MIM)
475 Riverside Drive, New York, NY 10115
Phone: (212) 870-3222
Fax: (212) 870-2765
www.moralityinmedia.org

National Coalition Against Censorship (NCAC)
275 Seventh Avenue, New York, NY 10001
Phone: (212) 807-6222
Fax: (212) 807-6245
www.ncac.org

National Law Center for Children and Families
3819 Plaza Drive, Fairfax, VA 22030
Phone: (703) 691-4626
www.nationallawcenter.org

National School Board Association
1680 Duke Street, Alexandria, VA 22314
Phone: (703) 838-6722
www.nsba.org

The Center for Democracy & Technology
1634 Eye Street NW, Suite 1100, Washington, DC 20006
Phone: (202) 637-9800
Fax: (202) 637-0968
feedback@cdt.org

The Classification and Rating Administration
15503 Ventura Boulevard, Encino, CA 91436
www.filmratings.com/questions.htm

Bibliography

Books

Anger, Kenneth. *Hollywood Babylon*. New York: Dell Paperbacks, 1981.

Brusendorff, Ova, and Paul Henningsen. *Love's Picture Book*: vol. 4, *The History of Pleasure and Moral Indignation*, translated by Elsa Gress. New York: Lyle Stuart, 1969.

Clark, Leta W. *Women, Women, Women: Quips, Quotes and Commentary*. New York: Drake Publishers Inc., 1977.

Cole, Lester. *Hollywood Red*. Palo Alto, CA: Ramparts Press, 1981.

Gravel, Senator Mike. *Introduction to The Pentagon Papers*, vol. 1. Boston: Beacon Press, 1971.

Hentoff, Nat. *Free Speech for Me—But Not for Thee*. New York: HarperCollins, 1992.

Knightley, Philip. *The First Casualty*. New York: Harcourt Brace Jovanovich, 1975.

Manchester, William. *American Caeser.* Boston: Little, Brown and Company, 1978.

Moore, Michael. *Stupid White Men.* New York: Regan Books of HarperCollins, 2001.

Morgan, Robin. *Going Too Far: The Personal Chronicle of a Feminist.* New York: Random House, 1977.

Schwartz, Bernard, and Lesher, Stephan. *Inside the Warren Court (1953–1969).* Garden City, New York: Doubleday & Company, Inc., 1983.

Siegel, Scott, and Barbara Siegel. *The Encyclopedia of Hollywood.* New York: Facts on File, 1990.

Sifakis, Carl. *The Encyclopedia of American Crime.* New York: Facts on File, 1982.

Strossen, Nadine. *Defending Pornography.* New York: Scribner, 1995.

Witt, Elder, ed. *The Supreme Court and Individual Rights.* Washington, DC: Congressional Quarterly Inc., 1980.

Woodward, Bob, and Scott Armstrong. *The Brethren: Inside the Supreme Court.* New York: Simon and Schuster, 1979.

Articles

Greenhouse, Linda. "An Intense Attack By Justice Thomas On Cross Burning," *The New York Times,* Dec. 12, 2002.

Janofsky, Michael. "Ban on Speaking Navajo Leads Café Staff to Sue," *The New York Times,* Jan. 20, 2002.

Lowenthal, David. "The Entertainment Industry Should Be

Censored," *Censorship*. Opposing Viewpoints. San Diego, CA: Greenhaven Press, Inc., 2002.

Moore, Frazier. "Revisiting the '60s and the Smothers Brothers Fight to Laugh About It." *Miami Herald*, Dec. 3, 2002.

Pitts, Leonard Pitts. "Ungodly Slaughter in God's Name," *Miami Herald*, Nov. 30, 2002.

Regaldo, Antonio, Gary Fields, and Mark Schoofs. "FBI Makes Military Labs Key Focus on Anthrax," *The Wall Street Journal*, Feb. 12, 2002.

Shesgreen, Deirdre. "Ashcroft Accuses Critics of Helping Enemy; He Rejects Complaints About Justice Department Actions," *St. Louis Post-Dispatch*, Dec. 7, 2001.

Siegel, Mark. "The Anthrax Fumble," *The Nation*, March 18, 2002.

Walker, William. "Rumsfeld charms the media while defending censorship," *Toronto Star*, April 11, 2002.

Web Sites

American Library Association
www.ala.org

Center for Constitutional Rights
openmedia@sevenstories.com

Eugene Weekly
www.eugeneweekly.com

National Center for Policy Analysis
www.ncpa.org

National Right to Life
www.nrlc.org

Office of the High Commissioner for Human Rights of the
United Nations
www.unhchr.ch/html

Parents Against Bad Books in Schools (PABBIS)
pabbis.com/news.htm

The Congressional Record
www.senate.gov

The New York Times Upfront
teacher.scholastic.com/upfront/issue7adebate.htm

The Reporters Committee for Freedom of the Press
www.rcfp.org

Index

Page numbers in **boldface** are illustrations, tables, and charts.

About the Author

Ted Gottfried has published more than twenty books for young adults, and nonfiction, novels, articles, and short stories for the adult market. Among his works are a six-book series on the Holocaust, a four-book series on the rise and fall of the Soviet Union, *Should Drugs Be Legalized?*, and *Alcohol* in the Marshall Cavendish Benchmark Drugs series. He has been a publisher, editor, and critic, and has taught writing courses at New York University and Baruch College. His wife, Harriet Gottfried, has recently retired from her position as director of training and development for the New York Public Library. He passed away before publication of this volume.